Alfred Plummer

The Church of the Early Fathers

External History

Alfred Plummer

The Church of the Early Fathers
External History

ISBN/EAN: 9783337162351

Printed in Europe, USA, Canada, Australia, Japan

Cover: Foto ©ninafisch / pixelio.de

More available books at **www.hansebooks.com**

THE CHURCH

OF THE

EARLY FATHERS

EXTERNAL HISTORY

BY

ALFRED PLUMMER, M.A., D.D.

MASTER OF UNIVERSITY COLLEGE, DURHAM
FORMERLY FELLOW AND TUTOR OF TRINITY COLLEGE, OXFORD

FOURTH EDITION

LONDON
LONGMANS, GREEN, AND CO.
AND NEW YORK: 15 EAST 16th STREET
1890

All rights reserved

PREFACE.

THE Christian Church has three ideals set before it in Scripture— to be Universal, to be Holy, and to be One. It is to 'make disciples of all the nations.' It is to be 'without spot or wrinkle or any such thing.' It is to 'become one flock' with a union between its members admitting of no lower standard than the Unity of the Divine Persons in the Godhead. The external history of the Church is the history of the attempt to realise the first of these three ideals; its internal history tells of the attempt to realise the second and third. The three taken together sum up what is meant by ecclesiastical history — the history of the spread of Christianity and of the development of Christian life and Christian doctrine. Thus a convenient division of the subject is at once suggested. Only the first of these three points is treated in this handbook— *the progress of the Church in the attempt to become universal*, including all that impeded that progress, especially literary attack and civil persecution. The worship and discipline of the Church and the development of its doctrine, though often touched upon, are reserved for treatment in a separate volume.

The present sketch is limited to the Ante-Nicene period, and indeed to only a portion of that. Neither the Apostolic Age nor the history of Arianism falls within its scope. Its limits are, roughly speaking, the second and third centuries, or, more exactly, the period from the death of St. John, about A.D. 100, to the Edict of Toleration published at Milan by Constantine and Licinius A.D. 312 or 313.

It is obvious that in a volume of this size nothing more than a sketch can be attempted; but help will be offered to the student who desires to have fuller information and to examine original sources for himself. A list is given of some of the best and most easily accessible authorities, especially in the English language, together with the chief ancient witnesses from whom the information given by modern writers is ultimately derived. Perhaps in no branch of history is it more important to study original authorities than in the history of Christianity during the second and third centuries. Neither in number nor in bulk are these sources so formidable as in the later periods of Church history; so that the ordinary student may hope to do a good deal in the attempt to make himself acquainted with primary materials. Moreover, nearly all these early writings have been translated; so that even those who are unable to read Latin or Greek are nevertheless able to obtain fairly accurate knowledge of what these early writers in their own words tell us. This handbook will have failed in one of its objects if it does not lead some of those who use it to check its statements by a comparison with standard works, and above all by an appeal to the original authorities.

As references are almost entirely forbidden by the plan of this series, the compiler of this volume is unable to express in detail his obligations to other writers. They are very numerous to a large number of the works mentioned below, especially to those of Bishop Lightfoot and Dr. Schaff, and to the ' Dictionary of Christian Biography' edited by Smith and Wace. An asterisk is prefixed to the name of modern writers whose writings are of special importance.

ORIGINAL SOURCES.

1. THE APOSTOLIC FATHERS.—Editions of Jacobson (1863), Gebhardt, Harnack, and Zahn (1876), Funk (1881). *Lightfoot's Clement (1869, 1877), Ignatius and Polycarp (1885). Translations in the *Ante-Nicene Library* (1868), and of portions by Hoole (1885).

2. THE APOLOGISTS AND OTHER CHRISTIAN WRITERS.— Greek: Justin Martyr, Irenæus, Clement of Alexandria, Hippolytus, Origen. Latin: Minucius Felix, Tertullian, Cyprian, Arnobius, Lactantius. Translations in the *Ante-Nicene Library* (1868-1872). Fragments of early Christian writers in Grabe's *Spicilegium Patrum* (1714), Routh's *Reliquiæ Sacræ* (1846-1848), Pitra's *Spicilegium Solesmense* (1852-1860), Bunsen's *Christianity and Mankind*, vols. v.–vii. (1854).

3. HEATHEN CONTROVERSIALISTS, whose works for the most part exist only in extracts: Lucian, Celsus, Porphyry, Hierocles.

4. CLASSICAL AUTHORS who notice Christianity: Pliny the Younger, Tacitus, Suetonius, Dion Cassius.

ANCIENT HISTORIANS.

GREEK.—Eusebius of Cæsarea. Translations of his *Eccl. Hist.* by Crusè (1838), in Bohn's *Ecclesiastical Library*, and in the *Greek Ecclesiastical Historians of the First Six Centuries* (1843-1847).

LATIN.—Rufinus (an inaccurate translation of Eusebius) and Jerome. The latter's *De Viris Illustribus* or *De Scriptoribus Ecclesiasticis* contains 135 Christian biographies from St. Peter to Jerome's own day; often very meagre, but of great value. From Jerome's translation and continuation of the *Chronicon* of Eusebius and from Rufinus's translation and continuation of his *Eccl. Hist.* Western Christendom during the Middle Ages derived most of its historical knowledge. See articles on these writers in the *Dict. of Christ. Biog.*, esp. that on Eusebius by Bishop Lightfoot.

MODERN WRITERS.

ENGLISH.—*Gibbon's *Decline and Fall of the Roman Empire*, esp. chaps. xv., xvi.; biassed against Christianity, but full of well-grouped information (best ed. Smith's Milman's, 1862). Kaye's *Eccl. Hist. of the Second and Third Cents. illustrated from Tertullian* (1845); also his *Justin Martyr* and *Clement of Alexandria*. Jeremie's *Hist. of Christ. Church in the Second and Third Cents.* (1852). Maurice's *Lectures on the Eccl. Hist. of the First and Second Cents.* (1854). Blunt's *Hist. of the Christ. Church during the first three Cents.* (1856). Pusey's *Councils of the Church from A.D. 51 to 381* (1857). Merivale's *Conversion of the Roman Empire* (1864). Milman's *Hist. of Christianity to the Abolition of Paganism* (1867). Mossman's *Hist. of the Cath. Church from the Death of St. John to the Middle of the Second Cent.* (1873). Neale's *Patriarchate of Antioch* (1873); also his *Hist. of the*

Eastern Church (1847). Newman's *Callis'a* (1873). Robertson's *Hist. of the Christ. Church*, vol. i. (1874). Mason's *Persecution of Diocletian* (1876). Crake's *Hist. of the Church under the Roman Empire* (1881). Wordsworth's *Church Hist. to the Council of Nicæa* (1881); also his *St. Hippolytus and the Church of Rome* (1881). Backhouse's and Tylor's *Early Church Hist.* (1884). *Schaff's *Hist. of the Christ. Church. Ante-Nicene Christianity* (1884).

TRANSLATIONS.—*Neander's *Church History* (1847). *Döllinger's *Gentile and Jew in the Courts of the Temple of Christ* (1862); and esp. his *Hippolytus and Callistus* (1876). Mosheim's *Institutes of Eccl. Hist.*, edited by Stubbs (1863). *Hefele's *Hist. of the Christ. Councils to the close of the Council of Nicæa* (1872). Baur's *Church Hist. of the first Three Cents.* (1878). *Uhlhorn's *Conflict of Christianity with Paganism* (1879). *Pressensé's *Early Years of Christianity* (1879).

FOREIGN.—*Le Quien's *Oriens Christianus* (1740). Morcelli's *Africa Christiana* (1817). Ritschl's *Entstehung der altkatholischen Kirche* (1857). *Keim's *Rom und das Christenthum* (1881). *Langen's *Geschichte der Römischen Kirche bis zum Pontificate Leo's I.* (1881); *Renan's *Marc-Aurèle* (1882); also his *L'Église chrétienne* (1879). Together with the elaborate works of the Centuriators of Magdeburg, of Baronius, Pagi, Tillemont, Fleury, and many others.

The spread of Christianity in the first three centuries is treated of by no contemporary writer. The passages bearing on the subject are for the most part general and more or less rhetorical statements—*e.g.* Pliny, *Epp.* x. 96 (the famous letter to Trajan); Ignatius, *Magn.* x.; Justin Martyr, *Try.* cxvii.; *Ep. ad Diognetum*, vi.; Minucius Felix, *Oct.* x. 33; Irenæus, *Hær.* I. x. 1, 2, III. iv. 2, V. xx. 1; Clement of Alexandria, *Strom.* VI. *sub finem*; Tertullian, *Adv. Jud.* vii., xii.; *Ad Scap.* ii., v.; *Apol.* i., xxxvii.; *Ad Nat.* I. viii.; *Adv. Marc.* III. xx.; Origen, *Con. Cels.* I. vii., xxvii., II. xiii., xlvi., III. x., xxiv., xxix., xxx.; *De Princip.* IV. i. 1, 2; Eusebius, *Hist. Eccl.* II. iii. 1, IV. vii. 1, VIII. i. 1, viii. 1, IX. ix. 14, X. iv. 17–20; Rufinus, *Hist. Eccl.* IX. vi. (Routh, *Rel. Sacr.* IV. pp. 6, 13).

CONTENTS.

CHAPTER I.
INTRODUCTORY.

Christianity the first universal religion—Evidence of its rapid growth—Criticism of the evidence—Work of the Apostles.   1

CHAPTER II.
THE CAUSES OF THE RAPID SPREAD OF THE GOSPEL.

Inadequacy of Gibbon's 'Five Causes'—Newman's criticism of Gibbon—Gibbon answered by Origen—Nine other causes—Three chief causes: 1. Sublimity of doctrine; 2. Boundless adaptability; 3. Divine origin   9

CHAPTER III.
THE CHURCHES IN SYRIA.

Obscurity of the Bishops of Jerusalem—Effect of Barcochba's revolt—Effect of the change of name—Bishops of Cæsarea—Influence of Origen and Eusebius—Ignatius of Antioch—His influence in ancient and modern times—Successors of Ignatius—Vagaries of Paul of Samosata—His condemnation and deposition—Appeal to Aurelian—Paul's successors—'School of Antioch'—Syrian text of Scripture . . .   21

CHAPTER IV.
THE CHURCHES IN ASIA MINOR.

Ephesus, the chief Church—Its position—Ignatius praises it—Polycrates and Victor—Polycarp of Smyrna and the Apostles—Polycarp and Ignatius—Epistle of Polycarp—His disciples

Irenæus and Florinus—Polycarp with Anicetus at Rome—His meeting with Marcion—His martyrdom—Its value as an example—Polycarp's successors—His companion Papias—Church of Hierapolis—Papias not an Ebionite, but an opponent of Gnosticism—Abercius of Hieropolis and his epitaph—Significance of the epitaph—Literary activity of Claudius Apollinaris, and of Melito of Sardis—Melito's Canon of the Old Testament—Influence of his writings—Asiatic evidence respecting the Fourth Gospel 35

CHAPTER V.

THE CHURCHES IN GREECE AND EGYPT.

Dionysius the Areopagite and his successors—Aristides the Apologist—Athenagoras the Apologist—Epistle of Clement to the Corinthians—Its significance—Testimony of Hegesippus—Epistles of Dionysius of Corinth—Bacchylus and the Easter question—Intellectual characteristics of Alexandria—The Alexandrian Schools—Catechetical School—Pantænus—Clement of Alexandria—He leaves Alexandria—His writings—His attitude towards pagan philosophy—His own philosophy and its defects—Greatness of Origen in his writings and in his life—His boyhood—His courage, industry, and indiscreet zeal—Visits to Rome, Arabia, and Palestine—Influence of Ambrose—Ordination and final departure from Alexandria—Work in Cæsarea—Martyrdom and death—Characteristics—Services to Christianity—Sources of his errors—Origen no heretic—Dionysius the Great—His letters—His defence of himself—His moderation—His successors—Conversion of Middle and Upper Egypt 54

CHAPTER VI.

THE CHURCHES IN ITALY.

Early Christianity Greek and uncentralised—Roman Christianity Greek in origin—Epistle of Clement—Epistle of Ignatius to the Romans—Visits of Hegesippus and Polycarp to Rome—Episcopacy in Rome promoted by heresy—Martyrs among the Bishops of Rome—Obscurity of the

CONTENTS xiii

PAGE

early Bishops—Nature of the appeals of Irenæus and of Tertullian—First Roman encroachment; Victor and Polycrates—The Roman writer Caius—Writings of Hippolytus —Relation to Tertullian and Origen—Hippolytus and Callistus—Death of Hippolytus—Martyrdom of Fabian— Roman see vacant—Novatian schism—Decline of Novatianism—Second Roman encroachment; Stephen and Cyprian—Alleged apostasy of Marcellinus—Fresh disturbances—Fictitious Councils—A *senatus* against Origen—A Council about the lapsed 87

CHAPTER VII.

THE CHURCHES IN NORTH AFRICA.

Origin of the African Church unknown—Province of Africa— Its prosperity—Characteristics of Carthage—Contrast with Alexandria—Its great men—Tertullian—His violent temper —The creator of ecclesiastical Latin—His chief writings— Tertullian the antithesis of Origen—First Council of Carthage—Cyprian's relation to Tertullian—Cyprian elected Bishop—Decian persecution—Cyprian's flight—His justification—Difficulties about the lapsed—Cyprian's troubles —Council of A.D. 252—Plague at Carthage—Question of rebaptizing heretics—Martyrdom of Cyprian—His greatness—Beginning of the Donatist schism—Arnobius . . 108

CHAPTER VIII.

THE CHURCHES IN GAUL AND BRITAIN.

Asiatic origin of the Gallican Church—Connexion of Irenæus with Asia and Gaul—His importance as a witness—Growth of the Gallican Church—Novatianism in Gaul—Persecutions—Influence of Constantine—The Church in Britain not founded by an Apostle—Bede's story of King Lucius; probably a fabrication—The British Church related to Gaul, confined to Roman settlements, small and poor— Distinct from the English Church 130

CHAPTER IX.

LITERARY CONTESTS WITH JEWS AND HEATHEN.

Hindrances to Christianity—Accusations by the heathen—Secular literature of the Church—Early apologies—Counter-accusations against paganism—Classification of the apologists—Greek and Latin apologists—The controversy with Judaism, with paganism—The pagan attack—The Christian reply, both defensive and offensive—The reply to heathen philósophy by Greeks and by Latins—The arguments from prophecy and from morality—Results of the apologies 144

CHAPTER X.

THE PERSECUTIONS.

The number of the persecutions indefinite—The chief causes: conservatism and fear—Limits to Roman toleration—Errors respecting 'the ten persecutions'—Crisis under Trajan—Its double aspect—Misconceptions respecting Hadrian and Antoninus—Tragic reign of M. Aurelius—Toleration under Commodus—Revival of paganism—Nature of the revival—Alternate persecution and peace—Un-Roman Emperors—Crisis under Decius—Christianity to be stamped out; if possible, without bloodshed—Wholesale apostasy—Flight and its consequences—Valerian turns persecutor—Formal toleration under Gallienus—Forty-five years of peace—New departure under Diocletian—His reconstruction of the Empire—He is led on to persecute: 1, by his own policy; 2, by the priests; 3, by the philosophers; 4, by Galerius and his mother—First edict of Diocletian—Two fires at Nicomedia—Second edict—Working of the two edicts—Third edict—Fourth edict—Abdication of Diocletian—Fifth edict—Galerius's edict of toleration—Close of the struggle—Edict of Milan—Number of martyrs—The Reign of Terror—The victory 1C0

CHRONOLOGICAL TABLES.

A.U.C.	A.D.	
851	98	Accession of TRAJAN.
	100	In September Pliny's *Panegyricus* addressed to Trajan.
	c 100	Death of St. John the Apostle.
	c 106	Martyrdom of Symeon, s. of Clopas, Bishop of Jerusalem, under the Proconsul Herodes Atticus.
	c.110	Alexander succeeds Euaristus as Bishop of Rome.
	111	Pliny becomes Proprætor of Bithynia.
865	112	Persecution of the Christians in Bithynia. Late in the year Pliny's *Letter to Trajan* (*Ep.* x. 97).
	c.112	Martyrdom of Ignatius at Rome, possibly Oct. 17. The *Epistles of Ignatius* were written one or two months before the martyrdom, and the *Epistle of Polycarp* one or two months after it.
	113	Column of Trajan dedicated. Trajan leaves Rome in the autumn for the Parthian campaign, and winters in Antioch. The interview with Ignatius at Antioch is a fiction.
	114	Trajan again winters in Antioch.
	115	Great earthquake in Antioch; Trajan injured.
	116	Revolt of the Jews in Cyrene, Egypt, and Cyprus.
870	117	The revolt quelled by Lusius. Trajan falls ill, sets out for Italy, and dies at Selinus in Cilicia, August 11. HADRIAN proclaimed Emperor by the army and accepted by the Senate.
	c.120	Xystus succeeds Alexander as Bishop of Rome.
	121	Hadrian visits Britain.
	c.124	Hadrian's *Rescript* to Minucius Fundanus, Proconsul of Asia, forbidding other than strictly legal proceedings against the Christians.
	c.126	Quadratus addresses his *Apology* to Hadrian.
	c.131	Death of Antinous and Birth of Irenæus. Papias completes his *Exposition of the Oracles of the Lord.*
885	c.132	Apotheosis of Antinous. A Roman colony planted at Jerusalem. The Jews refused admission.
	c.133	Aristides addresses his *Apology* to Hadrian. Revolt of the Jews under Barcochba.
	c.134	Hadrian's *Letter to Servianus.*
	135	Suppression of the Jewish revolt. Death of Barcochba. Jerusalem razed to the ground and rebuilt as a Roman city.
889	136	Jerusalem named Ælia Capitolina. The Christians return from Pella. Marcus becomes the first Gentile Bishop of Jerusalem.

A.U.C.	A.D.	
	c. 138	Martyrdom of Telesphorus, Bishop of Rome.
	138	Hadrian adopts Antoninus, Feb. 25, and dies at Baiæ, July 2.
		Accession of ANTONINUS PIUS.
	c. 140	*First Apology of Justin Martyr.*
895	c. 142	Pius succeeds Hyginus as Bishop of Rome.
		Shepherd of Hermas.
		So-called *Second Epistle of Clement.*
	c. 150	Birth of Tertullian.
	c. 151	Martyrdom of Publius, Bishop of Athens.
		Polycarp's visit to Anicetus, Bishop of Rome.
908	c. 155	Martyrdoms of Ptolemæus, Lucius, and others under Lollius Urbicus, City Prefect.
		Second Apology of Justin, and *Dialogue with the Jew Trypho.*
		Birth of Clement of Alexandria.
	155 or 156	} Martyrdom of Polycarp and his companions.
	c. 160	Montanus begins to prophesy.
		Octavius of Minucius Felix.
		Address to Greeks of Tatian.
		Commentary on St. John's Gospel by Heracleon.
914	161	Death of Antoninus Pius at Lorium, March 7.
		Accession of M. AURELIUS ANTONINUS and Association of L. Aurelius Verus (Ceionius Commodus) in the Empire.
		Birth of Commodus (the future Emperor), Aug. 31.
	c. 162	Martyrdoms of Felicitas and others under the City Prefect Publius [Salvius Julianus].
	c. 163	Martyrdoms of Justin and his companions under the City Prefect Q. Junius Rusticus.
	c. 164	Martyrdoms of Thraseas, Sagaris, and others.
920	c. 167	Lucian writes *De Morte Peregrini.* *Muratorian Canon.*
	c. 168	Soter succeeds Anicetus as Bishop of Rome.
	169	Death of the Emperor Verus late in the year.
	c. 173	Letters of Dionysius of Corinth to Soter and others.
	c. 174	War with the Quadi (*Legio Fulminata*). M. Aurelius writes his *Meditations.*
	c. 176	*Apology of Claudius Apollinaris.*
	c. 177	*Embassy* or *Apology of Athenagoras.*
		Eusebian *Apology of Melito.*
930	177	Bloody Persecution in Gaul. Martyrdoms of Pothinus, Blandina, Ponticus, and many others. Irenæus succeeds Pothinus as Bishop of Lyons, but probably later.
		Association of Commodus in the Empire.
	c. 178	Martyrdom of Cæcilia and her companions.
		Pantænus goes as a missionary to 'the Indians.'
	180	Theophilus of Antioch writes *Ad Autolycum.*
	180	Death of M. Aurelius in Pannonia, March 17. His persecuting policy survives him.
		Martyrdoms of Namphano and his three companions (the Medaurian Martyrs) at midsummer under the Proconsul Saturninus.
		Martyrdoms of Speratus and eleven others (the Scillitan Martyrs), July 17, under the Proconsul Saturninus.

CHRONOLOGICAL TABLES xvii

A.U.C.	A.D.	
933	180	COMMODUS returns to Rome as sole Emperor. The Persecutions cease.
	c. 180	Pantænus becomes Head of the Catechetical School at Alexandria.
	183	Plot of Lucilla and Quadratus against Commodus, and promotion of the φιλόθεος παλλακή Marcia. She secures the peace of the Christians.
	c. 185	Birth of Origen. Conversion of Tertullian to Christianity. Irenæus completes his work *Against Heresies*.
	c. 186	Martyrdom of the Senator Apollonius.
942	189	Demetrius succeeds Julianus as Bishop of Alexandria.
	c. 190	Clement succeeds Pantænus as Head of the Catechetical School, writes the *Address to Greeks*, and soon afterwards the *Pædagogus*. Callistus is recalled from exile in the mines of Sardinia through the influence of Marcia.
945	192	Commodus assassinated in the night of Dec. 31.
	193	PERTINAX proclaimed Emperor, Jan. 1; assassinated Mar. 28. The Empire put up to auction and sold by the Prætorians to DIDIUS JULIANUS. SEPTIMIUS SEVERUS proclaimed Emperor in Pannonia, Apr. 13; Julianus executed, June 2.
	198	Caracalla associated with his father in the Empire.
	c. 200	Tertullian becomes a Montanist. Birth of Cyprian.
955	202	Renewed persecution of the Christians. Martyrdoms of Perpetua, Felicitas, and others at Carthage; of Leonides, father of Origen, at Alexandria.
	c. 203	Clement withdraws from Alexandria and is succeeded in the Catechetical School by Origen.
	204	Imprisonment of Clement's pupil, Alexander, afterwards Bishop of Jerusalem.
	c. 204	Zephyrinus succeeds Victor as Bishop of Rome.
	208	Severus in Britain with his sons.
	209	Geta associated in the Empire.
	c. 210	Apollonius of Ephesus writes against Montanism.
	211	Severus dies at York, Feb. 4. CARACALLA and GETA return to Rome. Clement of Alexandria sent by Alexander, still in prison, to Antioch: the last notice of Clement.
965	212	Geta assassinated late in February. Alexander, released from prison, visits Jerusalem, and is translated to that see as coadjutor of Narcissus: the first instance of translation.
	c. 213	Origen visits Rome in the pontificate of Zephyrinus.
	c. 215	Origen, driven from Alexandria, settles at Cæsarea. Syriac *Apology of Melito*.
970	217	Caracalla assassinated, Apr. 8. MACRINUS proclaimed Emperor, Apr. 11.
	218	Macrinus defeated and slain by Julia Mæsa and Elagabalus.
	219	ELAGABALUS goes to Rome and is accepted as Emperor.

C.H. a

A.U.C.	A.D.	
	c. 219	Callistus succeeds Zephyrinus as Bishop of Rome. Origen returns to Alexandria.
	c. 220	Alcibiades publishes the *Book of Elkesai* in Rome. Synod at Carthage under Agrippinus decrees the rebaptism of heretics.
	221	Julius Africanus publishes his work on chronology.
975	222	Elagabalus slain, Mar. 11. Accession of ALEXANDER SEVERUS.
	c. 222	Urban succeeds Callistus as Bishop of Rome. Heraclas, Origen's convert, associated with him in the Catechetical School. Paschal Cycle of Hippolytus constructed.
	c. 228	Origen ordained presbyter at Cæsarea by Theoctistus of Cæsarea and Alexander of Jerusalem.
	c. 229	Origen returns to Alexandria and writes *De Principiis*.
	c. 230	Synods at Iconium and Synnada decree the rebaptism of heretics. Pontian succeeds Urban as Bishop of Rome.
894	231	Origen finally leaves Alexandria. Two Synods at Alexandria under Demetrius condemn him. Heraclas succeeds him as head of the Catechetical School.
	233	Heraclas succeeds Demetrius as Bishop of Alexandria.
	235	Alexander Severus and his mother slain in Gaul. MAXIMIN the Thracian, the first barbarian Emperor, elected by the troops in Gaul. Persecution of the Christians. Pontian banished with Hippolytus to Sardinia: Anteros succeeds him. Origen takes refuge with Firmilian in Cappadocia, and writes *On Martyrdom* to Ambrose and Protoctetus in their imprisonment.
	236	Fabian succeeds Anteros as Bishop of Rome.
990	c. 237	Gregory Thaumaturgus writes his *Panegyric on Origen*. Correspondence between Julius Africanus and Origen.
	238	Insurrection in Africa under the Gordians. Maximin and his son slain at Aquileia in May. The third GORDIAN accepted by the Senate and Prætorians in July.
	c. 240	Gregory Thaumaturgus ordained Bishop of Neo-Cæsarea.
	c. 244	Synod at Bostra to try Beryllus; he is reclaimed by Origen.
997	244	Gordian slain in Mesopotamia. PHILIP the Arabian concludes a shameful peace with Sapor and returns home.
	245	Birth of Diocletian.
	c. 245	Origen completes the *Hexapla*. He corresponds with the Emperor and his wife Severa.
1000	c. 247	Dionysius succeeds Heraclas as Bishop of Alexandria.
	248	Philip celebrates the 1000 years of Rome.
	c. 248	Cyprian ordained Bishop of Carthage.
	249	Origen writes *Against Celsus* at Cæsarea. Philip marches against Decius and is slain near Verona, June 17.
	249	DECIUS revives the Censorship and appoints Valerian to the office.
	250	Edict against Christianity. General Persecution.

CHRONOLOGICAL TABLES xix

A.U.C.	A.D.	
		Martyrdoms of Fabian and many others. The see of Rome vacant for sixteen months.
	251	Synod at Carthage in April about the *lapsi.* It condemns Novatian.
		Synod at Rome under Cornelius excommunicates Novatian.
		Correspondence between Cornelius and Fabius of Antioch.
		Decius slain in a campaign against the Goths.
		GALLUS elected Emperor. He revives the Persecution.
1005	252	Synod at Antioch condemns Novatianism.
		Cornelius retires from Rome and dies, Sept. 14.
	253	Lucius succeeds him and is succeeded by Stephen.
		Gallus slain by his own troops.
		VALERIAN elected Emperor: he associates his son Gallienus with him in the Empire.
		Death of Origen.
	c. 255	Synods at Carthage under Cyprian decree the rebaptism of heretics against Stephen of Rome.
		Birth of Arius the heresiarch.
	256	Novatian writes *De Trinitate.*
	c. 256	Valerian renews the Persecution.
1010	257	Dionysius banished from Alexandria.
		Xystus II. succeeds Stephen.
	258	Martyrdoms of Xystus II., Aug. 6, of Laurence, Aug. 10, and of Cyprian, Sept. 14.
	259	Dionysius succeeds Xystus.
	260	Paul of Samosata elected Bishop of Antioch.
	c. 260	Birth of Eusebius of Cæsarea.
	260	Valerian taken prisoner by Sapor.
	261	GALLIENUS makes Christianity a *religio licita.*
1015	262	Martyrdom of Marinus at Cæsarea.
	c. 264	Synod at Antioch under Firmilian to try Paul of Samosata.
		Porphyry at Rome with Plotinus.
	265	Maximus succeeds Dionysius at Alexandria.
1020	c. 267	Second Synod at Antioch against Paul.
	268	Gallienus slain at Milan in March.
	269.	CLAUDIUS defeats the Goths in Dardania.
		Firmilian dies at Tarsus on his way to the Third Synod at Antioch against Paul.
		Felix succeeds Dionysius at Rome and condemns Paul.
	270	Claudius dies at Sirmium.
1025	272	AURELIAN, appealed to by the Church, executes the sentence of the Synod against Paul.
	c. 272	Porphyry writes *Against Christians.*
	c. 273	Suppression of the Kingdom of Palmyra.
	c. 274	Birth of Constantine.
	275	Aurelian slain in the spring.
	276	TACITUS dies in Asia Minor, Apr. 9.
1035	282	PROBUS slain at Sirmium.
	283	CARUS dies in the East.
	284	DIOCLETIAN elected Emperor. 'The Era of the Martyrs.'
	286	MAXIMIAN associated in the Empire.
1045	292	Constantius and Galerius become Cæsars.
	303	First Edict against Christianity, Feb. 23.
		Diocletian visits Rome to celebrate his Vicennalia.

CHRONOLOGICAL TABLES

A.U.C.	A.D.	
	804	Fourth Edict, making Christianity a capital offence. The see of Rome vacant for thirty-one months.
	805	Abdications of Diocletian and of Maximian. Maximin Daza and Severus become Cæsars.
	806	Death of Constantius at York in July. SEVERUS becomes Emperor, Constantine becomes Cæsar. MAXENTIUS is proclaimed Emperor, and MAXIMIAN resumes the purple.
1060	807	Severus slain. CONSTANTINE made Emperor by Maximian, LICINIUS by GALERIUS; MAXIMIN DAZA assumes the title of Emperor.
	c. 308	Edict against the Manicheans.
	308	Fifth Edict against Christianity.
	310	Maximian hanged.
	311	Galerius publishes an Edict of Toleration, Apr. 30, and dies in May.
1065	812	Cycle of *Indictions* begins, Sept. 1. Maxentius defeated at the Milvian Bridge by Constantine, Oct. 28.
	312 or 313	} Edict of full Toleration published at Milan.

The succession of the Bishops of Jerusalem and Ælia will be found pp. 21-23; of the Bishops of Antioch, pp. 29-33; of the Bishops of Alexandria, pp. 63, 86. In the following table of the Bishops of Rome the succession only is given as certain; the chronology down to Dionysius (A.D. 259-269) is for the most part tentative, and even after that date is not always secure:—

BISHOPS OF ROME.

A.U.C.	A.D.		A.U.C.	A.D.	
820	67	Linus.		236	Fabian, martyred 250.
	79	Cletus, Anacletus, or Anencletus.			See vacant for 16 months.
	91	Clement.		251	Cornelius.
	100	Euaristus.			[Novatian, Antipope.]
	110	Alexander.		253	Lucius.
	120	Xystus or Sixtus I.		253	Stephen.
	128	Telesphorus, martyred.	1010	257	Xystus or Sixtus II., martyred 258.
	138	Hyginus.			
895	142	Pius.			See vacant.
	150	Anicetus.		259	Dionysius.
	168	Soter.		269	Felix.
	177	Eleutherus.		275	Eutychian.
	190	Victor.		283	Gaius or Caius.
	204	Zephyrinus.		296	Marcellinus.
	219	Callistus or Calixtus. [Hippolytus, Antipope.]			See vacant for several years.
			1060	307	Marcellus.
975	222	Urban.		309	Eusebius.
	230	Pontian, died in exile.			See vacant.
	235	Anteros.		311	Miltiades or Melchiades.

THE CHURCH

OF

THE EARLY FATHERS.

CHAPTER I.

INTRODUCTORY.

'WHERESOEVER the Bishop shall appear, there let the people be; just as wheresoever Jesus Christ is, there is the Universal Church.'

In this exhortation of Ignatius to the Church of Smyrna (the earliest passage extant in which the expression 'Universal Church' occurs) the original meaning of 'universal' or 'catholic,' as applied to the Church, is evident. However true it may be to say that the real sign of the supremacy of the Christian society is, not that it spreads everywhere, but that it embraces the whole truth, yet as regards the history of the term 'catholic' the primary reference is to the universality of the extension of the Church, and not to the comprehensiveness of its teaching. Ignatius is distinguishing between each local church, of which the bishop is the head, and the Universal Church, of which Christ is the Head. The expression occurs again in the inscription to the 'Martyrdom of Polycarp' (c. A.D. 156), and twice in the body of the narrative; and in each case the explanation 'throughout every place' or 'throughout the whole world' accompanies it (see p. 42). Its meaning, therefore, is indisputable. As Augustine says, the Church is called καθολική in Greek, *quod per totum orbem terrarum diffunditur.*

The word 'universal' was not new; it occurs in Polybius, Philo, and elsewhere. But as an epithet of a religion, or of a religious body, it was entirely new. All religions previous to Christianity were national or state religions. Each tribe, country, and government had its own gods and its own forms of worship. Religion, so far from drawing nations together, kept them more sharply divided. It was an additional barrier to be surmounted or swept away before union was possible. No doubt one people sometimes borrowed a deity or a ceremonial from another; but that no more created a religious union between the two than the reception of refugees created a political union. In the very nature of things it is impossible that any form of polytheism can become universal. If a plurality of gods is once admitted, each nation and class will choose its own divinities. A religion that aspires to become universal must at least have risen to the truth that there is but one God; and the only religion which before the birth of Christ had attained to this truth had cut itself off from all others, only fitfully making, or attempting to make, converts. The purest religion which the world had yet seen was also the most exclusive. Thus, while the Gentile always

Marginal note: Christianity the first universal religion

lacked the power, the Jew often lacked the will, to make his faith and worship universal.

Christianity from the outset was endowed with both. Its Founder came 'to draw *all* men' unto Himself, and commissioned His followers to teach all 'that repentance and remission of sins should be preached in His Name unto *all* the nations;' and to ensure success He promised them 'power from on high,' and to be with them Himself 'alway, even unto the end of the world.' The will and the power to make the new faith coextensive with the human race were granted from the outset: and the history of the Apostolic Age is the history of the first response to that endowment. It is a history which, so to speak, runs underground. We read it, as we read the geological history of this planet, rather in its effects than in its operations. The same forces are working now as were working at the outset; but the conditions have enormously changed. Yet there is 'the record of the rocks' to teach us what the operations of natural forces in prehistoric ages must have been. And there are the records of the second and third centuries to teach us what the operations of spiritual forces in the Apostolic Age must have been. Of the labours of all but two or three of the Apostolic band we know scarcely anything. If we set aside the traditions of later ages, most of the Twelve are mere names to us. And even these traditions are in the majority of cases very meagre. Of the history of Christianity in general during the half-century after the death of St. Paul we have scarcely any details. But what it must have been we see clearly from the state of things which is implied in the writings of Pliny,

Evidence of its rapid growth

Ignatius, and Justin Martyr, of Irenæus, Clement of Alexandria, and Tertullian.

Within fifteen years of the death of St. John, Pliny informs Trajan that in his province of Bithynia 'many of every age, *every rank*, and also of both sexes, are called into danger and are likely to be so; and not only through the cities, but even through the villages and rural districts, the contagion of that superstition has spread.' And we have no reason to suppose that Christians were more numerous in Pontus and Bithynia than in other parts of Asia Minor at that time. Some ten or fifteen years later Ignatius speaks of Christianity as that 'wherein *every tongue* believed and was gathered together into God.' About the middle of the century, and therefore only fifty years after the close of the Apostolic Age, Justin Martyr declares that, widely dispersed as is the Jewish race, yet there are nations into which no Jew has ever been; whereas 'there is *not one single race of men*, whether barbarians or Greeks, or whatever they may be called, nomads, or vagrants, or herdsmen living in tents, among whom prayers and giving of thanks are not offered through the Name of the crucified Jesus.' The date of Minucius Felix is disputed, but, assuming that Tertullian borrowed from him, and not he from Tertullian, we may with Bishop Lightfoot date the 'Octavius' c. A.D. 160. In it we read: 'Let us not flatter ourselves on our numbers. *We seem to ourselves to be many;* but in the sight of God we are very few.' Passing over about twenty years we come to the great work of Irenæus 'Against Heresies,' written between A.D. 175 and 190. The first two passages come from the portion of Book I., which (thanks to Epiphanius) we possess in the original Greek as well as in the Latin translation. 'For the Church, although *dispersed throughout the whole world even to the ends of the earth*, has received from the Apostles and their disciples the belief in one God.' . . . 'This preaching and this faith, as we said before, the Church, although *dispersed in the whole world*, carefully guards, as if housing in one house.' Later on he says that '*many nations* of those barbarians who believe in Christ' assent to the authority of Apostolic tradition: and again that 'the path of those who are of the Church *circumscribes the whole world.*' A few years later than this we have almost simultaneously the evidence of Clement of Alexandria and Tertullian. Clement, after pointing out how limited were the efforts, and still more limited the successes, of the Greek philosophers, continues: 'But the word of our Master remained not in Judæa alone, as philosophy did in Greece, but was diffused *over the whole world*; among Greeks and barbarians alike, nation by nation and village by village, and in every city, persuading whole families and hearers one by one, and already winning over to the truth not a few of the philosophers themselves.' Tertullian speaks of Christians being '*almost a majority* in every city,' and asks Scapula 'What will you do with so many thousands of human beings, such multitudes of men and women, of every sex and every age and *every rank*, when they give themselves up to you?' In a famous passage in his treatise 'Against the Jews' he speaks of *Britannorum inaccessa Romanis loca, Christo vero subdita*, and of 'many remote nations, and many provinces and islands, to us unknown, and which we can scarce enumerate: in all which places the Name of the Christ who is already come reigns.' Against Marcion he urges: 'Behold whole nations emerging from the whirlpool of human error to God the Creator, to God the Christ. . . . Christ who has now taken the whole world with the faith of His Gospel.' But perhaps no passages are more often quoted in this connexion than two in the 'Apologeticus': 'Their outcry is that the State is besieged; that Christians are in the fields, the fortresses, the islands; they lament as a dire calamity that every sex, age, condition, and even rank, is going over to this profession.' And again: 'We are a people of yesterday, and we have filled everything of yours—cities, islands, fortresses, towns, councils, your very camps, tribes, companies, palace, senate, forum. We have left you nothing but your temples. We can count your armies, and our numbers in a single province will be greater.' The more temperate author of the 'Epistle to Diognetus' writes: 'What soul is in body, Christians are in the world. The soul is diffused through all the members of the body: Christians are scattered through all the cities of the world.'

Let us frankly admit that Pliny's informants may have exaggerated the case, or that he himself in his Criticism of perplexity has given a highly coloured account the evidence of the facts; that Ignatius is using the language of hope or prophecy rather than of history, and that he may even have Is. xlv. 23 in his mind; that Justin Martyr, Irenæus, and Clement are manifestly stating more than they could with any certainty know; and that Tertullian is a rhetorician, who delights in sweeping statements, and does not shrink from giving mere rumours as if they were indisputable facts. Nevertheless, when we have made all reasonable abatement from any or all of these statements, we shall find that there is an irreducible minimum of very large amount. Something not very much less than what is told us by these writers is required to account for the panic and frenzy with which the heathen themselves, and especially the Roman Government, regarded the new religion, and to explain the early date of its final success. In much less than three hundred years from the death of St. John, the Roman Empire was nominally Christian. We need these statements—almost in their literal meaning—in order to bridge over the gulf between Domitian and Constantine. Even in Domitian's time there were not only slaves and freedmen 'of Cæsar's household' to send Christian greetings to their brethren elsewhere; that was already possible under Nero; but the *superstitio nova ac malefica* had reached the Imperial family itself. Flavius Clemens, Domitian's own cousin and colleague in the consulship, whose children were heirs designate to the throne, was a Christian. His wife, Flavia Domitilla, another cousin of the Emperor, was a Christian also; and she and her husband were among the first sufferers in the persecution under Domitian: she, by banishment to an island, and he by death. It is a step further when Ignatius expresses a fear that there are Christians in Rome who have influence enough to obtain the Imperial pardon for him, and thus deprive him of the glory of martyrdom. But even thus we are far from the point when the Roman Emperor himself summoned Councils and enforced their decrees (Arles, A.D. 314; Nicæa, A.D. 325). As Eusebius says of the latter Synod, 'the whole thing seemed to be a dream rather than a reality.' The statements, therefore, of Justin Martyr, Irenæus, Clement, and Tertullian, do not much more than give as a fact a condition of things which we should have to assume as an hypothesis, in order to account for the ultimate triumph of the new religion just three centuries after the death of its Founder.

This career of rapid success implies a great deal as to the work of the first band of preachers. The 'underground' work of the Apostles must have been both wide and deep to have rendered such success, humanly speaking, possible. It is a case in which ἀρχὴ πλεῖον ἢ ἥμισυ παντός ('Well begun is more than half done') seems pre-eminently true. The details of their work are almost wholly unknown to us; but of its thoroughness and extent we can judge from its results. We can put little trust in the traditions which assign definite fields of labour to the different Apostles: Thrace and Scythia to Andrew, Parthia to Philip, Armenia and Arabia Felix to Bartholomew, Ethiopia to Matthew, India to Thomas, Egypt and Mauretania to Simon, Arabia and Persia to Jude. The traditions are for the most part late, and by no means harmonious. But something not very different from this must have been done, and well done, either by the Apostles or by their immediate disciples. The rapid progress of the Gospel during the period of which this volume has to treat, implies much previous labour by men whose very names are for the most part unknown to us.

CHAPTER II.

THE CAUSES OF THE RAPID SPREAD OF THE GOSPEL.

GIBBON'S 'Five Causes of the Growth of Christianity' have passed into a commonplace: (1) the zeal which the early Christians inherited from the Jews; (2) the doctrine of the immortality of the soul and of future rewards and punishments; (3) the miraculous powers claimed by the primitive Church; (4) the morality of the early Christians; (5) their well-ordered ecclesiastical organisation. But it was long ago pointed out by Milman that in these celebrated fifteenth and sixteenth chapters Gibbon has confounded the origin and first propagation of Christianity with its later progress. Its divine origin is for the most part eluded by the device of beginning the account in the second or third century instead of in the first. The failings of Christians in these and later ages are introduced in order to insinuate a doubt as to the purity, and therefore as to the divine character, of the Gospel. Yet these chapters will probably never lose their interest (and, if we discount the sneering tone, they will never lose their value) as a masterly exposition of important facts.

[margin: Inadequacy of Gibbon's 'Five Causes']

But they need to be supplemented or prefaced by a statement of what Gibbon chooses to ignore. The causes enumerated to a large extent explain the rapid success of the Gospel; but *they do not explain themselves.* Self-sacrificing zeal, sublime beliefs, and pure morality are not ultimate facts of human nature; nor are they so common as not to call for investigation. They are themselves effects of some cause or causes; and the philosophic historian is bound to enquire into their origin. The triumphant zeal of the first Christians is intelligible, if we remember that it was zeal for a Divine Person. If this fact is omitted, how are we to account for the contrast between its speedy and permanent victory and the comparative failure of all other enthusiasms? The conquest of the Christian doctrine of immortality over other forms of the same belief is intelligible, if we remember its connexion with Him who died, and rose again, and liveth for evermore. Otherwise, why should the Christian have succeeded where the Pharisee and the Platonist failed? The morality of the Gospel is at once recognised as sublime by all serious men; and its superiority in this respect to the very best teaching which the world had previously received is intelligible, if we remember that it proceeded from Him who not only spake as never man spake, but was Himself sinless and divine. And the success of the early Christians in following His moral teaching is intelligible, if we remember that they made the attempt relying on the promised help of their Master, and not on the strength of their own wills. But how is the immeasurable superiority of Christian ethics to be explained, if the Author of them was a mere man? And allowing, for the sake of argument, that the Sermon on the Mount does not soar much higher than the best teaching of psalmists, prophets, and philosophers, how was it that many Christians reached a standard of life never attained by the Stoic or the Jew? To supply lofty moral teaching is one thing; to induce men to follow it is quite another.

It is not enough to tell us that the virtues of the early Christians go a long way towards explaining their success as propagandists. Whence, in an age of boundless immorality, came their lofty moral standard and the ability to live up to it?

Dr. Newman in his 'Grammar of Assent' subjects Gibbon to criticism from another point of view. 'He thinks these five causes, when combined, will fairly account for the event; but he has not thought of *accounting for their combination*. If they are ever so available for his purpose, still their availableness arises out of their coincidence ; and out of what does that coincidence arise ? Until this is explained, nothing is explained, and the question had better have been left alone. These presumed causes are quite distinct from each other, and, I say, the wonder is, what made them come together. How came a multitude of Gentiles to be influenced by Jewish zeal ? How came Zealots to submit to a strict, ecclesiastical *régime* ? What connexion has such a *régime* with the immortality of the soul ? Why should immortality, a philosophical doctrine, lead to a belief in miracles, which is a superstition of the vulgar ? What tendency had miracles and magic to make men austerely virtuous ? Lastly, what power had a code of virtue, as calm and enlightened as that of Antoninus, to generate a zeal as fierce as that of Maccabæus ? Wonderful events before now have apparently been nothing but coincidences, certainly ; but they do not become less wonderful by cataloguing their constituent causes, unless we also show how they came to be constituent.'

Newman's criticism of Gibbon

But, after all, says Dr. Newman, the main question

is not how the causes came to be combined, but whether they are adequate to the effect. Did these five characteristics of Christianity cause the conversion of bodies of men to the Christian faith? And he answers this question emphatically in the negative.

1. 'Christians had zeal for Christianity after they were converted, not before.'

2. 'Certainly in this day there are persons converted from sin to a religious life by vivid descriptions of the future punishment of the wicked; but then it must be recollected that such persons already believe in the doctrine. . . . The thought of eternal glory does not keep bad men from a bad life now, and why should it convert them then from their pleasant sins to a mortified existence, to a life of ill-usage, fright, contempt, and desolation?'

3. 'A claim to miraculous power on the part of the Christians, which is so unfrequent as to become an objection to the fact of their possessing it, can hardly have been a principal cause of their success.'

4. Gibbon himself says of the primitive Christians that 'their gloomy and austere aspect, their abhorrence of the common business and pleasures of life, and their frequent predictions of impending calamities, inspired the Pagans with apprehension of some danger which would arise from the new sect.' On which Dr. Newman remarks: 'We have here plain proof that the Christian character repelled the heathen; where is the evidence that it converted them?'

5. 'As to the ecclesiastical organisation, this, doubtless, as time went on, was a special characteristic of the new religion; but how could it directly contribute to

its extension? Of course it gave it strength, but it did not give it life. . . . It is one thing to make conquests, another to consolidate an empire.'

There is, in fact, no escape from the position which Origen about A.D. 250 took up against Celsus. 'In all <small>Gibbon</small> Greece, and in all barbarous races within our <small>answered by Origen</small> world, there are tens of thousands who have left their national laws and customary gods for the law of Moses and the word of Jesus Christ; though to adhere to that law is to incur the hatred of idolaters, and to have embraced that word is to incur the risk of death as well. And considering how, in a few years and with no great store of teachers, in spite of the attacks which have cost us life and property, the preaching of that word has found its way into every part of the world, so that Greeks and barbarians, wise and unwise, adhere to the religion of Jesus—*doubtless it is a work greater than any work of man.*' This hypothesis accounts for the facts. Will any other hypothesis do so equally well?

We may say, then, of Gibbon's five causes: (1) that they are themselves effects as well as causes, and therefore require explanation; (2) that their combination needs to be explained; all the more so as some of them are not obviously very harmonious; (3) that even when combined they do not seem to cover all the facts, for some of them, by repelling instead of attracting converts, would often conduce to failure rather than to success.

Let us, therefore, after accounting for the five causes and their combination by recognising the divine origin of Christianity, supplement them by some further considerations. And first let us go outside Christianity and consider the condition of the world during the time that the Gospel was winning its way through all ranks of society to the Imperial throne. There were various circumstances which very materially assisted its progress.

<small>Nine other causes of the success of Christianity</small>

1. The *destruction of Jerusalem* had rendered the keeping of the Mosaic Law in its entirety a physical impossibility. Judaism, though it continued for some time longer to be a harassing enemy, had ceased to be a possible rival. No heathen, with the claims and conditions of both before him, could doubt whether the Law or the Gospel had the better hope to offer to him.

2. The splendid *organisation of the Roman Empire*, with its facilities for travel, correspondence, and commerce, supplied a ready-made machinery for the propagation of the faith.

3. The *destruction of nationalities* by Roman conquest was another preparation. The idea of a religion not national but universal would have seemed monstrous to the rugged and exclusive patriotism of an earlier age.

4. The dissolution of nationalities was accompanied by a *dissolution of creeds*. The more thoughtful, who regarded polytheism as incredible, took refuge in a vague Monotheism, which, although it was powerless to give life to worship or purity to morals, nevertheless prepared the way for the truth.

5. The Macedonian conquest had done something towards making mankind familiar with a *type of civilisation* which seemed capable of becoming universal. All through the known world there were Greeks and

Hellenized barbarians exhibiting a common standard of culture and social morality.

6. *Roman Law*, originally intensely national and exclusive, had gradually become almost coextensive with the civilised world. All freemen throughout the empire were made Roman citizens. Tribal and national ideas about the powers of fathers over sons, husbands over wives, and masters over slaves, gave place to principles of natural right and universal justice. Roman Law, like the Mosaic Law, became a *pædagogus* to lead mankind to Christ.

7. The *worship of the Roman Emperor*, although in one way a hideous obstacle to Christianity, in another way acted as its forerunner. It was nominally universal. It was the one form of worship which was coextensive with the Empire. And it was heartiest and most real in the provinces, in which the Emperor was personally unknown. In it the provinces gave honour to the power to which they owed peace, security, and civilisation. It was possible to transfer to the true Author of all good this reasonable feeling of gratitude.

8. The *prevalence of the Greek tongue* in all the great cities and in many of the country districts of the Empire rendered the New Testament in the original language almost everywhere intelligible. Teaching and exposition were facilitated by the same fact. Nearly every one knew either Greek or Latin, and very many knew both. With these two languages the Gospel could be preached almost throughout the whole civilised world. And the Latin Version of the New Testament was one of the earliest, if not the very earliest, that was made.

9. *Pagan society was hopelessly corrupt*, and religion,

philosophy, and statecraft had all proved utterly powerless to reform it. In the contest between *religion* and vice, it was vice that had forced religion to become its servant, rather than religion that had conquered, or even checked, vice. Lust and bloodshed were consecrated as worship, and the gods were adored in mysteries that were only too fitly described as 'unspeakable.' Nor did *philosophy*, while hastening the downfall of the popular religion, do anything to improve public morality. Sceptical and materialistic in tone, it doubted or denied the existence of a spiritual world and the value of moral virtue. Even Stoicism, which was the most serious and positive form of philosophic belief, left the masses untouched, and did but little for the cultivated. It made a few wealthy persons live less luxuriously than they would otherwise have done: but this advantage was counterbalanced by the impulse given to intellectual and spiritual pride. The Stoic aimed at being not so much the servant of God as His equal. Nor could philosophy give any relief to the profound misery of an accusing conscience, unable to purify itself from sin or to conquer temptation. Society tried to drown the reproachful voice in noise, or to contradict it by insisting on man's glorious achievements. But below this self-assertion lay the conviction that man had been made for better things and was going on irretrievably from bad to worse. *Statecraft* had been equally unsuccessful. As soon as he was safely established on the throne, Augustus had played the part of a pious ruler, and had endeavoured to revive something of primitive simplicity and virtue. He built and restored temples; he made reforms in legislation; he patronised the respectable and frowned on the openly dissolute; he enlisted the chief literary men of the age in the attempt to reform it. And all in vain. Temples rose most rapidly just as the beliefs which they represented were passing most surely away. The public and private scandals of the Emperor's own life neutralised his legislation. The moral teaching of the leading writers was in like manner vitiated by themselves. Horace at his best was met by Horace at his worst. And what chance, in that evil age, had the purity of Virgil against the unblushing licentiousness of Ovid? Most men remained of Ovid's opinion. They preferred the existing dissipation to the ancient simplicity which Augustus thought it politic to restore.

*Prisca juvent alios: ego me nunc denique natum
Gratulor: hæc ætas moribus apta meis.*

Men who had proved by bitter experience that neither government, nor speculation, nor the worship of rival deities, had any remedy or consolation for the intolerable evils of the time, were sometimes thereby prepared for the good news of the Gospel.

But had the circumstances of the time been twice as favourable as they were to the reception of Christianity, its success would have been small and transient had it not possessed in itself the characteristics of a universal religion. These are mainly three : (1) incomparable sublimity of doctrine; (2) inexhaustible adaptability to different ages, nationalities, classes, and individuals; (3) an origin recognisable as divine. The first two necessarily involve the third. Neither the one nor the other can be satisfactorily

Three chief causes

accounted for, unless the Gospel is, what it professes to be, a revelation. Nothing less than a supernatural origin can account for its immeasurable superiority in these two respects. Human intelligence is not an adequate cause. And this superiority is proved not merely by the success of the Gospel, but by the fact that it has never been superseded. 'In a moral point of view,' says Goldwin Smith, 'the world may abandon Christianity, but it can never advance beyond it. This is not a matter of authority, or even of revelation. If it is true, it is as much a matter of reason as anything in the world.' Christianity, when it comes in contact with heathen civilisations, absorbs their better elements and leaves the rest to decay. They never prove themselves to be superior to it.

1. Let us assume, for the sake of argument, what is in itself absolutely incredible, that the Carpenter of Nazareth was learned in all the wisdom of the Orientals, Greeks and Romans; that He had opportunities of studying the teaching of Confucius, Zoroaster, and the Vedas, of Æschylus, Plato, and Aristotle, of Lucretius, Cicero, and the Stoics; and that He made use of all or some of these in preparing the Gospel. Is this composition of causes adequate to the effect? Will any eclecticism, working on these materials, give us the Sermon on the Mount or the discourses in the Fourth Gospel? Above all, will any compound of ancient philosophy account for the life of Christ and the lives of His followers? *Purpurei panni* taken from a multitude of systems could never make a satisfying Gospel. Such things are interesting to the philosophic moralist and lawyer; but they are not the materials

1. Sublimity of doctrine

out of which an edifice that is to shelter humanity can be made. The superiority of the teaching of Christ to the sum of all that is noblest in all His predecessors is admitted; and it is a characteristic which was necessary to the foundation of a religion for all mankind. A mere eclectic system could never inspire even widespread enthusiasm.

2. But it is its inexhaustible adaptability to the infinite varieties of human life which specially marks the Gospel as a universal religion. By countless experiments century after century it has proved its congruity with the aspirations, not of any sect or nation or age, but of the spiritual nature of man. Under the most various conditions of prosperity and misery, of peace and war, of wealth and poverty, of civilisation and barbarism, of culture and ignorance, of race, period, climate, government, age, and sex, it has been recognised as furnishing the supreme type of moral excellence and the best satisfaction of man's spiritual needs. Nor is this all. It is the one religion which has proved liberal enough and strong enough to adopt and to keep whatever was worth gaining and preserving among the forces with which it has come in contact. Without this power of expansion and assimilation, no religion can become universal, and hence the failure of some of the best religious systems. There are whole races of men which Judaism and Mahometanism through long ages of intercourse have failed to attract. There are whole continents to which Buddhism remains not only unadapted but unintelligible. Can we point to any race or class of men to whom Christianity has proved spiritually unsuitable? Other types

2. Boundless adaptability

of moral excellence contain peculiarities which sooner or later prove fatal to their being accepted as universal or final. The Christian type has been preserved from all such things. Neither the heroic is sacrificed to the beautiful, nor the beautiful to the heroic: there is equal scope for reverence and love. Its virtues are neither masculine nor feminine. They exhibit none of the special characteristics of Pharisee or Sadducee, of Jew or Gentile, of Roman or Greek. They bear no impress of the political or social peculiarities of Palestine at the time when they were first given to the world as a standard. 'The essence of man's moral nature, clothed with a personality so vivid and intense as to excite through all ages the most intense affection, yet divested of all those peculiar characteristics, the accidents of place and time, by which human personalities are marked—what other notion than this can philosophy form of Divinity manifest on earth?'

3. The question is a just one. The inexhaustible adaptability of the Gospel can be adequately explained only on one hypothesis—that its origin is divine. Its authority in this respect was felt, even when not definitely recognised as binding. It was not only as being 'new' that the teaching of Christ excited amazement, but as being 'with authority,' and not like the traditional and formal morality of the scribes. In a far deeper sense than that in which the officers of the Sanhedrin used the words, the experience of centuries affirms the declaration, 'Never *man* so spake'—Οὐδέποτε ἐλάλησεν οὕτως ἄνθρωπος.

<small>3. Divine origin</small>

CHAPTER III.

THE CHURCHES IN SYRIA.

THE Church of *Jerusalem*, 'the mother of all the Churches,' is remarkable in history rather for what it has suffered than for what it has done. Jew, Roman, Christian, Persian, Arab, and Turk, one after another, have had possession of the city. Its eminence among the Churches resulted from its hallowed situation rather than from the activity of its members or the ability of its bishops. Little is known of it during the second and third centuries. It produced no one during that period who either as a leader or as a theologian has left a name in history. Its second bishop, Symeon, son of Clopas, suffered martyrdom by torture and crucifixion at the age of a hundred and twenty under Atticus, A.D. 107, and was succeeded by Justus, who is also called Judas. Then follow Zacchæus, Tobias, Benjamin, John, Matthias, Philip Seneca, Justus II., Levi, Ephres, Joseph, and Judas. All these bishops were Jews by birth, as the names of most of them indicate. They bring us down to the defeat and death of Barcochba, and to the rebuilding of Jerusalem by the Romans, as Ælia Capitolina. Marcus, the first Gentile bishop, succeeded as bishop of Ælia, A.D. 136, and is said to have suffered martyrdom under Antoninus Pius, c. A.D. 155. Then follow Cassianus, Publius, Maximus, Julian, Gaius, Julian II., Capito (Maximus II., Antoninus), Valens, Dolichianus, and Narcissus. False charges were laid against Nar-

[margin: Obscurity of the bishops of Jerusalem]

cissus, and he retired into the wilderness, the see being held meanwhile by Dius, Germanion, and Gordius. When the charges were disproved, Narcissus returned. He is said to have presided over a Synod of fourteen bishops at Jerusalem to consider the Easter controversy. His colleague and successor is something more than a name. The lifelong friendship of Alexander with Origen began when they were students together under Pantænus and Clement at Alexandria. Alexander became bishop of some town in Cappadocia, and was in prison as a confessor from A.D. 204 to 211. On his release he visited Jerusalem, where he was chosen as coadjutor to the aged Narcissus. This was a double transgression of ecclesiastical rules, which forbade translations and ordered that no city should have more than one bishop. But a Synod summoned for the purpose ratified the arrangement (A.D. 213); and on the death of Narcissus Alexander became sole bishop. His episcopate is remarkable for the excellent library which he formed at Jerusalem, of which Eusebius made much use in writing his history, and for his staunch friendship with Origen, whom he ordained presbyter. Alexander was a second time a confessor in the Decian persecution, and died in prison, A.D. 251. Eusebius has preserved some fragments of Alexander's letters, *e.g.* some words of warm affection and admiration addressed to Origen; and part of a letter addressed to Demetrius of Alexandria in defence of his own conduct in joining with Theoctistus of Cæsarea in getting Origen, while still a layman, to preach in the presence of bishops. Alexander was followed by Mazabanes, Hymenæus (A.D. 266), Zabdas (298), Hermon (302), and Macarius (311). The long episcopate of Hymenæus covers thirty-two very eventful years; but of his share in the history of the time we know little beyond the fact that he took a leading part in the proceedings at Antioch (264-269) against Paul of Samosata. The service-books of the Greek Church state that Hermon sent missionary bishops to the barbarians in the Crimea; but neither Eusebius nor Jerome seems to know of this. Macarius lived to attend the Council of Nicæa, and it was during his episcopate that Helena, the mother of Constantine, made her celebrated pilgrimage to Jerusalem.

During this long and obscure period in the history of the Mother Church of Christendom there is one crisis which yields results of importance— *Effect of Barcochba's revolt* the Jewish revolt under Barcochba. The rebellious Jews persecuted the Christians of Palestine with the utmost animosity. From their point of view the Jewish Christians were traitors to the national cause. But the Christians had their own way of resisting and defeating the Roman Empire; not by revolt, but by martyrdom. In this case they became martyrs *for* Rome, and suffered rather than rebel against their persecutor. The effect of this Jewish persecution was to place a sharp and final line of demarcation between the Church and the Synagogue. Even the heathen now began to see that the Christians were not a Jewish sect. When Hadrian's new city was opened on the ruins of Jerusalem, Christians, whether of Jewish or Gentile origin, were allowed to enter, while Jews were excluded. The Jewish Christian who still clung to Judaism had to separate himself more and more widely from his Christian brethren, and under the name of Ebionite went outside the Church.

With the loss of the old name the Church of Jerusalem lost its rank and importance. The bishop of Ælia became a mere suffragan of the metropolitan of Cæsarea. This position continued until the fifth century, when the crafty and ambitious Juvenal succeeded in getting his see erected into a patriarchate. But during this long interval the sacred associations of the city caused it gradually to recover its primitive dignity, so that it ranked almost as the equal of its own metropolitan. The seventh canon of Nicæa points to this condition of things. 'Whereas custom and ancient tradition have ordained that the bishop of Ælia should be honoured, let him have the honorary precedence (τὴν ἀκολουθίαν τῆς τιμῆς); but without prejudice to the proper dignity of the metropolitan see.' Not until after the Council of Nicæa does the name of Jerusalem come into use again. Eusebius speaks sometimes of Ælia and sometimes of Jerusalem.

Effect of the change of name

Bishops of Cæsarea

The origin of the metropolitan Church of *Cæsarea in Palestine* is unknown. Turris Stratonis first became of importance under Herod the Great, who made 'temples of Cæsar' (Καισαρεῖα) here as well as at Cæsarea Philippi and Samaria. This worship of himself Augustus permitted in the provinces, if combined with the worship of Rome. Vespasian made Cæsarea a Roman colony without the *jus Italicum*, and Tacitus calls it *caput Judææ*. Alexander Severus or his successors allowed it the title of *metropolis*, a designation which appears on coins. The population

THE CHURCHES IN SYRIA 25

was pagan, with a sprinkling of Jews. Figures of Zeus, Poseidon, Apollo, Heracles, Dionysus, Athene, Nike, and Astarte occur on the coins of Cæsarea in the second and third centuries. While the situation of Jerusalem kept it aloof from the world, that of Cæsarea placed it in close connexion with the great centres of commerce and civilisation. So important a city would be likely to have a bishop at an early date. The 'Apostolic Constitutions' give Zacchæus the publican as the first bishop, and Cornelius, who is perhaps meant for the centurion, as the second. We are on much firmer ground when we come to Theophilus, whom Eusebius mentions as contemporary with Narcissus of Jerusalem, c. A.D. 190. He is said to have presided over a Synod of twelve bishops on the Paschal question. He was followed by Theoctistus, who with Alexander of Jerusalem commissioned Origen while still a layman to expound scripture in church, and afterwards ordained him, in defiance of his own bishop, Demetrius of Alexandria. This was c. A.D. 228. Some thirty years later he was succeeded by Domnus, who was very quickly followed by Theotecnus. It was Theotecnus who encouraged the distinguished soldier Marinus to become a martyr A.D. 262. As Gallienus had previously recognised Christianity as a religion which might be tolerated, it is possible that Marinus suffered as an offender, not against religion, but against military law. Or he may have been persecuted by the rebellious Macrianus, who deliberately transgressed the indulgent edict of Gallienus. Theotecnus also took a prominent part in the proceedings against Paul of Samosata. His successor Agapius ordained Pamphilus, the great friend of

Eusebius, presbyter. Eusebius knew him, and praises his affectionate care for the smallest details in his diocese. Probably Eusebius himself was ordained presbyter by Agapius, for Agapius was the immediate predecessor of Eusebius. Baronius, Le Quien, and others give Agricolaus as the successor of Agapius and predecessor of Eusebius, but Agricolaus was bishop of Cæsarea in Cappadocia. The fact that Eusebius mentions no such person as his predecessor is almost conclusive.

The chief points of interest in the history of the Church of Cæsarea during this period are the residence of Origen there (first between A.D. 215 and 219 and again after his final departure from Alexandria in 231), the education of Eusebius, the foundation of the great library by Pamphilus, and the martyrdoms during the Diocletian persecution. Most of these will come before us again in other connexions, but they require mention here. It would be difficult to over-estimate the effect of what they imply on the Church at large. Had the work of Origen, Pamphilus, and Eusebius at Cæsarea remained unrecorded, there would be a huge blank in ecclesiastical history rendering much that is otherwise known scarcely intelligible. Had that work never been done, the course of ecclesiastical history would have been very different. In the whole of the second and third centuries it would be difficult to name two more influential Christians than Origen and Eusebius; and Pamphilus laboured earnestly to preserve and circulate the writings of the one and to facilitate those of the other. It was from the libraries of Pamphilus at Cæsarea

Influence of Origen and Eusebius

and of Alexander at Jerusalem that Eusebius obtained most of his materials.

From the second metropolis of Palestine we pass to the second metropolis of the Christian Church. While Cæsarea succeeded Jerusalem as the political capital of Palestine, *Antioch* succeeded it as the centre of Christendom. The magnificence, luxury, and shameless licentiousness of Antioch have been often described, both by ancient and modern writers, and need be no more than mentioned here. Its suburb Daphne, even in that land and age, was a marvel for its beauty and immorality. It was at Antioch that Christians first received their name, probably in mockery, from the heathen rabble, who made even emperors wince with their sharp tongues. But there is a tradition preserved by John Malalas that Euodius, the first bishop of Antioch and immediate predecessor of Ignatius, originated the name. Euodius is a mere name; but the fact of his presidency is sufficiently attested, and may be placed about A.D. 50–70. The history of the see of Antioch begins with the Ignatian Epistles, written shortly before the martyr's death. Of the episcopate of Ignatius, which may be assumed to have lasted from about A.D. 70 to about 112, we know absolutely nothing until the saint receives sentence of death, and begins to write his farewell letters on his journey to Rome to be executed by the beasts in the Flavian amphitheatre. This sentence shows that he was not a Roman citizen. A Roman would have been beheaded as was St. Paul. And the eagerness with which he anticipates it (Rom. i., ii., v., &c.) shows that he went to Rome, not like St. Paul to appeal to Cæsar, but to be made a victim in the bloody sports of the arena. He was escorted by 'ten leopards,' as he calls the soldiers who guarded him. They took him from Troas across the Ægean to Neapolis in Thrace, and thence to Philippi, where we lose sight of him. 'Rome was at length reached. In the huge pile, erected for the colossal display of these inhuman sports by the good emperors of the Flavian dynasty, Ignatius, the captain of martyrs, fell a victim under the good emperor Trajan. Tragic facts these, on which it is wholesome to reflect.'

More than a century before the Church of Cæsarea illuminated Christendom through the teaching of Origen, the Church of Antioch supplied the influence of this great martyr's death to the Church. The influence was all the more impressive from the suddenness of its appearance. It was 'as the lightning coming forth from the East and seen even unto the West.' This saintly bishop, of whom few had heard before, suddenly became the central figure in Chritsendom. In his martyr's progress from East to West he visits Churches, and is visited by solemn deputations from them. His last written words to them are treasured up as spiritual heirlooms, to teach whole generations of Christians what the true faith is, and with what joyous enthusiasm they must welcome the honour of dying for it. And the sincerity of the teaching is guaranteed by the death of the man who taught it. For three centuries after his death his seven brief letters served two great purposes—to protect the belief in the reality of Christ's humanity as well as in His Divinity, and to encourage Christians to suffer death for their creed. During the last three centuries

His influence in ancient and modern times

THE CHURCHES IN SYRIA 29.

they have served as one of the chief defences of the episcopal form of Church government. For this reason their authenticity has been frequently challenged, but may now be considered as finally established through the works of Zahn and Bishop Lightfoot.

The successor of Ignatius in the see of Antioch was Hero. One of the spurious Ignatian letters, supposed to have been written by the martyr from Philippi, is addressed to him, and Baronius quotes as genuine an address of Hero to Ignatius which is 'manifestly of a later age.' Hero is said to have suffered martyrdom A.D. 129, and was succeeded by Cornelius, who was followed by Eros c. A.D. 143. The fifth bishop of Antioch is the apologist Theophilus, whose letters to the heathen scoffer Autolycus are still extant. He is the first Christian writer who uses the term 'Trinity' ($\tau\rho\iota\acute{a}s$), and who quotes St. John *by name*. His episcopate may be placed A.D. 168–186. He must be distinguished from his contemporary, Theophilus of Cæsarea. He was followed by Maximinus ('H. E.' IV. xxiv.) and c. A.D. 199 by Serapion. The latter wrote against Montanus and on the apocryphal Gospel of Peter which was in use in his diocese at Rhossus in Cilicia. A fragment of the latter treatise is preserved by Eusebius, and is important as showing with how much independence the canon of Scripture was determined in different Churches. That the various centres arrived in the main at the same result is a strong guarantee of the correctness of that result. Asclepiades, a confessor during the persecution under Severus, followed c. A.D. 203–218. Alexander, then a bishop of Cappadocia, and afterwards bishop of Jeru-

Successors of Ignatius

salem, wrote to congratulate the Church of Antioch on having such a pastor. Clement of Alexandria was the bearer of the letter, and it is the last historical notice that we have of Clement. Philetus and Zebennus follow as bishops of Antioch, and then we once more meet a famous name in Babylas, c. A.D. 238-251. His fame is threefold. He is said to have anticipated St. Ambrose in repelling an emperor from the Church until he had done penance for some deed of blood. He was a martyr in the Decian persecution. And his relics caused the confusion of the Emperor Julian, A.D. 362. His successor Fabius was disposed to favour the Novatian cause, and had a correspondence with Cornelius, bishop of Rome, on the subject. Dionysius of Alexandria also wrote to him on the subject of the *lapsi* and of the martyrs of Alexandria. It is important to notice that the decision of the bishop of Rome respecting Novatus and Novatian was not regarded as conclusive by the Church of Antioch. A Synod was summoned to consider the question, to which Dionysius of Alexandria was invited by the bishops of Tarsus, of Cæsarea in Palestine, and of Cæsarea in Cappadocia. But Fabius died before the Synod met, and was succeeded by Demetrianus. Under Demetrianus the Synod was held which decided against Novatianism, A.D. 252. The death of Fabius was fatal to the chances of Novatianism in the East; but we need not suppose that, with the whole case before him, he would have favoured it against the convictions of all his colleagues and suffragans.

The successor of Demetrianus was the notorious Paul of Samosata. The character of his heresy will be considered in another volume. Here only the main

THE CHURCHES IN SYRIA 31

facts of his episcopate will be noticed. Samosata, which had already (c. A.D. 120) produced Lucian, 'the Vagaries of Voltaire of the second century,' now sent forth Paul, 'the Socinus of the third,' to perplex the Church by leading the great see of Antioch into heresy. He is an early instance of those prelates who, by pomp, luxury, and lax morality, have been among the chief scandals of Christianity. If in doctrine Paul anticipated Socinus, in life he anticipated Pope Alexander VI. Eusebius gives the details of his conduct as sketched by the third Synod which condemned him. He was *Ducenarius procurator*, or Chancellor under the Empire, and was also a sort of viceroy to Zenobia, Queen of Palmyra, to whose dominions Antioch then belonged; and he adopted the life and state of a civil governor rather than those of a bishop. Even in church he was still the Roman official with a *tribunal* and railed-off *secretum* for his use. His sermons were popular orations, which the congregation were expected to applaud by clapping and waving of handkerchiefs. He abolished the hymns in honour of Christ as being 'modern compositions' (νεωτέρους καὶ νεωτέρων ἀνδρῶν συγγράμματα), and at Easter introduced female choristers to sing in honour of himself. This perhaps refers to the practice, which Jerome mentions with disapproval, of greeting bishops with Hosannas. The fifty-ninth canon of the Synod of Laodicea forbade the public use of hymns composed by private individuals; but it is very doubtful whether this aimed at innovations such as those introduced by Paul at Antioch. Paul was also accused of unseemly familiarity with young women, and of corrupt practices both as a magistrate and as a bishop. He began life in great poverty, and by some means acquired an amount of wealth which was remarkable even in wealthy Antioch.

Three Councils sat to consider his case. In 264 or 265 Gregory Thaumaturgus and his brother Athenodorus, His condemnation and deposition Firmilian of Cæsarea in Cappadocia, Theotecnus of Cæsarea in Palestine, Hymenæus of Jerusalem, Helenus of Tarsus, Maximus of Bostra, and many others, argued and remonstrated with Paul in many sessions. He sophistically disclaimed the heresies imputed to him, and satisfied the Synod of his orthodoxy. But his teaching soon compelled them to meet again at Antioch. Paul promised to retract, and the Synod again accepted his statements. At both these Councils Firmilian seems to have presided. He died on his way to the third in 269, and Helenus presided. This Synod was a very large one, consisting of seventy or eighty bishops, besides other clergy. The presbyter Malchion was selected, like the deacon Athanasius at Nicæa, to take the lead in the disputation. Paul was convicted, deposed, and excommunicated; and Domnus, son of his predecessor Demetrian, was chosen to supersede him. An encyclical was sent to Rome, Alexandria, and other Churches, announcing the results of the Synod, but in no way submitting them for revision, or asking for confirmation. The quotations from the encyclical given by Eusebius do not contain any explanation of the fact that the Council condemned the very term afterwards adopted at Nicæa—$\dot{o}\mu oo\acute{v}\sigma\iota os$. Probably Paul had used this term in some very misleading sense.

Paul refused to submit to the decree of deposition or to vacate the episcopal residence. The Church at last appealed to the Emperor; and Aurelian, having conquered Paul's patroness Zenobia, decided against him, A.D. 272. Aurelian decreed that the ecclesiastical fabrics at Antioch belonged to the bishop who was recognised as such by the bishops of Italy and Rome. This is the first instance of an ecclesiastical appeal to the civil power, an appeal all the more remarkable because the civil power was not yet Christian. A hostile heathen Emperor aided the Church to execute its own decrees. The principle on which he acted was intelligible and natural. Italy and Rome were the centre of the Empire; and the Christian officials in Italy and the metropolis would be pretty sure to judge rightly in the case in question. At any rate, their opinion was a fair guide to the opinion of the majority of Christians throughout the Empire. It is incredible that Aurelian knew anything of a supremacy of the Roman see. If so, why mention the bishops of Italy?

Appeal to Aurelian

Domnus, appointed by the Synod, but not elected by the Church of Antioch, did not hold the see long. Of course Paul's supporters rejected him, and even some of the orthodox held aloof on account of the disregard of the rights of the clergy and laity of Antioch, which had been shown in appointing Domnus. He was followed in A.D. 274 by Timæus, and in 283 by Cyril. It was under Cyril, whom Eusebius speaks of as a contemporary, that Dorotheus attained such fame as a Hebraist and interpreter of Scripture. Cyril was succeeded by Tyrannus, who was bishop during the Diocletian persecution, which he outlived, A.D. 303–314.

Paul's successors

Not until a little later did the Church of Antioch reach the zenith of its prosperity. St. Chrysostom was born there A.D. 347; and it was in his time that Antioch, with its hundred thousand Christians, became the leading Church in Asia, especially in the Arian controversy, for Arianism was very prevalent there. But all this lies outside our period.

The so-called 'School of Antioch' has its origin just before the close of our period. Dorotheus, mentioned above, and the martyr Lucian may be regarded as its founders. In contrast to the allegorising mysticism of the School of Alexandria, it was distinguished by a more sober and critical interpretation of Scripture. It looked to grammar and history for its principles of exegesis. But we must not suppose that there was at Antioch an educational establishment like the Catechetical School at Alexandria, which, by a succession of great teachers, kept up a traditional mode of exegesis and instruction. It was rather an intellectual tendency which, beginning with Lucian and Dorotheus, developed in a definite direction in Antioch and other Syrian Churches.

'School of Antioch'

The study of Scripture in the Syrian Church resulted in a special type of *text* which is commonly known as Syrian. This Syrian text (called by Bengel 'Asiatic,' and by Griesbach 'Constantinopolitan' or 'Byzantine') is represented by Codex A in the Gospels, by the Peshitto, Chrysostom, and most cursives. It is the basis of the so-called *Textus Receptus*, which is now admitted to be very corrupt.

Syrian text of Scripture

These notices of the Churches of Jerusalem, Cæsarea in Palestine, and Antioch must suffice as representative of the Syrian Churches. The number of these Churches was considerable even in the second century, and by the beginning of the fourth was very large indeed, as is seen by the number of bishops who attend local Councils. A detailed account of the bishops of each see, so far as any notice of them survives, will be found in the pages of Le Quien. The Syriac Version of the Scriptures was one of the earliest translations made, and at Edessa we have the first instance of a Christian dynasty.

CHAPTER IV.

THE CHURCHES IN ASIA MINOR.

WHY 'the Seven Churches of Asia' are selected for special notice in the Apocalypse is not easily determined. Even at that early date they were not the only Christian congregations in Asia Minor; and so far as we know there were Churches at least as important as some of those included among the seven. For a long time after that date Asia Minor continued to be the part of the world in which Christians were most numerous. But from every point of view any account of the spread of Christianity in Asia Minor must give the chief place to Ephesus.

<small>Ephesus, the chief Church</small>

The Church of *Ephesus*, with St. Paul as its founder and Timothy as its overseer, was honoured in having the last of the Apostles as its guardian and adviser during the latter portion of his life. After Jerusalem and Antioch it became the third centre of Christianity. With its mingled population of Asiatics and Greeks, it combined more completely than any other city the cha-

<small>Its position</small>

racteristics of both East and West; and in its commercial and intellectual activity it was admirably suited for being the headquarters of missionary enterprise and doctrinal development.

After the death of St. John, Ephesus becomes prominent again during the journey of Ignatius to his martyrdom at Rome. His letter to the Ephesian Church is the longest and most elaborate of the seven. He did not pass through Ephesus, but the Ephesians sent a deputation headed by their Bishop Onesimus to visit the saint at Smyrna; and from Smyrna he wrote the letter. He writes of the Ephesian Church as 'renowned unto all ages.' No heresy, had found a home there. It was steadfast in doctrine and discipline. But there are enemies (the Docetic Gnostics) close at hand who must be shunned as wild beasts. By public worship 'within the precinct of the altar' and by submission to their unassuming bishop, they will avoid the danger; above all, 'breaking one bread, which is a medicine of immortality, and an antidote against (spiritual) death.' He promises to write to them again; but this promise he was probably prevented from fulfilling.

Ignatius praises it

After Onesimus we have no conspicuous person among the bishops of Ephesus until near the end of the second century, when Polycrates and his celebrated controversy with the imperious Victor of Rome about the Quartadecimans—the second outbreak of the Easter question (see p. 40). Of the numerous Councils held on the subject at that time, all but that presided over by Polycrates agreed that the Resurrection must be celebrated on no other day but Sunday. Poly-

Polycrates and Victor

crates—in a letter preserved by Eusebius—defends the Asiatic custom by an appeal to ancient and constant tradition, including Philip, John, Polycarp, and seven relations of Polycrates himself, all of whom had been bishops. 'And, having been sixty-five years in the Lord, he is not alarmed by threats.' Victor of Rome made a vain attempt to declare those who followed the Ephesian Synod in this matter excommunicate, the first attempt made by the Church of Rome to dictate to other Churches. It failed, in spite of the excellence of Victor's cause, and the immense majority on his side. Irenæus, in this a true son of peace, interposed and reproved Victor for his undue severity towards Polycrates. Thus early does the solidarity of the widely scattered Churches become evident. A bishop of Gaul prevents a rupture between the bishops of Rome and Syria and the bishops of Asia Minor. The fact that the Quartadeciman practice about Easter was becoming connected with Montanism probably led Victor into his ill-advised attempt to secure uniformity. Jerome admires the *ingenium et auctoritatem* of Polycrates.

Whether Apollonius, who wrote a considerable work against Montanus and his prophetesses c. A.D. 210, was bishop of Ephesus, or even a member of the Ephesian Church, as the author of 'Prædestinatus' states, is doubtful. Eusebius, who quotes from his work, is silent on the point. So also is Jerome. Tertullian thought the book worthy of an answer in his Περὶ ἐκστάσεως, which is no longer extant.

During the next hundred years the Church of Ephesus produced no famous bishop or theologian.

The great glory of the Church of *Smyrna* is the martyr Polycarp, the disciple of St. John the Apostle, and the master of Irenæus of Lyons. The worthlessness of the 'Life of Polycarp,' which professes to have been written by Pionius, has been shown by Bishop Lightfoot and others. ' Of the real Polycarp we know very little—far too little to satisfy our interest, though somewhat more than is known of any eminent Christian from the age of the Apostles to the close of the second century.' He was born about the time, perhaps in the very year, of the destruction of Jerusalem, and of Christian parents—according to the most natural interpretation of his own language at his martyrdom. As a boy he may have known Andrew and Philip, who, like St. John, appear to have taken up their abode in Asia Minor, Andrew at Ephesus and Philip at Hierapolis. But the statement of Irenæus, that Polycarp was 'instructed by Apostles' (ὑπὸ ἀποστόλων μαθητευθείς) need not mean more than that he was the disciple of one of the Twelve. For Irenæus states also that Polycarp was appointed bishop in Smyrna 'by Apostles.' This could hardly be before Polycarp was at least twenty-five (c. A.D. 95), at which date it is practically certain that St. John was the only surviving Apostle. This means that Polycarp was bishop of Smyrna for over fifty years; for St. John died c. A.D. 100, and the martyrdom of Polycarp is now securely fixed at A.D. 155 or 156. Irenæus also tells us that Polycarp was the companion of another pupil of St. John, viz. Papias, and though the statement may be a mere inference, it has probability on its side.

In his Epistle Polycarp shows knowledge of the

Epistle of Clement of Rome to the Corinthians: but that he knew Clement himself, or had corresponded with him, is nowhere stated, and is not probable.

On the other hand, that Polycarp was personally known to Ignatius is beyond reasonable doubt. Igna-
<small>Polycarp and Ignatius</small> tius halted in Smyrna on his way to be martyred at Rome, and in the letters which he wrote from Smyrna to the Churches of Ephesus and Magnesia he speaks of his love for Polycarp and of the comfort which Polycarp is to him; and from Troas he wrote not merely to the Church of Smyrna, but to Polycarp individually. In the latter letter stands the prophetic admonition: 'Stand firm as an anvil under the stroke. It is the part of a great athlete to be smitten and conquer.'

Ignatius went on to Philippi, and there charged the Church to send tidings to Antioch. The charge led to
<small>Epistle of Polycarp</small> the production of one, and the preservation of another, of the most precious relics of the sub-Apostolic age. The Philippians wrote to Polycarp and begged that the messenger from Smyrna to Antioch might carry their letter. Polycarp replied in the epistle which is still extant, and with his own letter sent copies of all those of Ignatius which had come into his hands. As he asks for news of Ignatius, it is evident that his letter to Philippi was sent before news of the death of Ignatius had reached Asia Minor. The date of Polycarp's letter depends upon the date of the martyrdom of Ignatius; probably c. A.D. 112.

Whether Melito, Claudius Apollinaris, Polycrates, and Justin Martyr were personally known to Polycarp is uncertain; but such men would be likely to seek out a pupil of the Apostle St. John. That Irenæus, the opponent, and Florinus, the victim, of Gnosticism, were among the personal disciples of Polycarp is known to us from the writings of the former. In rebuking Florinus for his wild opinions, he reminds him of the days when they both of them listened to the teaching of Polycarp, as he rehearsed what he had heard from John and others respecting the teaching of Christ (see p. 132). And it is by no means improbable that Pothinus, the martyred predecessor of Irenæus in the see of Lyons, may have been another disciple of Polycarp.

<small>His disciples Irenæus and Florinus</small>

Towards the end of his life Polycarp visited Rome and discussed the Paschal question with Anicetus. Each appealed to tradition; the Bishop of Rome to the practice of his predecessors almost from apostolic times, who had always commemorated the Crucifixion on a Friday, and the Resurrection on a Sunday; the Bishop of Smyrna to the practice of St. John and other Apostles, who had always celebrated the Christian Passover on the 14th Nisan, without regard to the day of the week. Unlike his successor Victor, Anicetus made no attempt to coerce Polycarp and the Asiatic Churches, though he could not convince him. On the contrary, he allowed him to celebrate the Eucharist in his place; and they parted with mutual affection.

<small>Polycarp with Anicetus at Rome</small>

It was perhaps at Rome that Polycarp had his encounter with the heresiarch Marcion. 'Recognise us,' said the latter. 'I recognise the firstborn of Satan,' was the reply; stern words, which remind us of his master's declaration, 'In this the children

<small>His meeting with Marcion</small>

of God are manifest, and *the children of the devil,*' and ' he that doeth sin *is of the devil.*' To this latter passage, combined with 1 John iv. 2, 3, Polycarp evidently alludes in his letter to the Philippians.

Soon after his return from Rome he obtained the martyr's crown. The annual festival was being celebrated at Smyrna under the Asiarch Philip, and the proconsul Statius Quadratus was present. A persecution was in progress, and eleven Christians had been thrown to the wild beasts. A cry was raised for Polycarp. He left the city, and might have escaped when his retreat was discovered. But he submitted to what he believed to be the will of God, and was taken back to the city. Quadratus urged him to swear by the genius of Cæsar and cry 'Away with the atheists!' Polycarp solemnly repeated, 'Away with the atheists!' The proconsul, seeming to have gained half his point, cried, 'Swear, and I will set thee free. Revile Christ.' Then came the famous answer, on the interpretation of which the chronology of much of Polycarp's life depends, 'Four score and six years have I served Him, and He has done me no wrong. How then can I speak evil of my King, who saved me?'

The games with beasts were over, and the Asiarch refused to have Polycarp exposed to the lion. The crowd then shouted that he should be burnt. And this was done. The flames at first refused to touch him, and made a canopy over him; and the attendant then stabbed him. The Christians were prevented by the Jews from obtaining the corpse, and it was consumed on the fire. But they were allowed to gather up the bones. It is said that Irenæus, then in Rome, was mysteriously informed of his master's death. At the moment when Polycarp passed away he heard a trumpet voice proclaiming, 'Polycarp has been martyred.' The Church of Smyrna, in the account of the martyrdom which it sent to the Church of Philomelium and 'to all the brotherhoods of the holy and *universal Church* Its value as an example sojourning in every place,' expresses its belief that nearly all this came to pass that the Lord might show us once more an example of martyrdom which is *conformable to the Gospel. For he waited to be delivered up,* even as the Lord did, that we too might become imitators of him, not looking only to that which concerns ourselves, but also to that which concerns our neighbours: for it is the mark of true and sure love not only to desire that oneself be saved, but all the brethren also.' This probably alludes to the selfish and presumptuous conduct of a fanatical Phrygian named Quintus, who without waiting to be accused forced others to come forward with himself and profess themselves Christians. When he saw the wild beasts he turned coward and sacrificed. 'For this cause therefore, brethren, we praise not those who *give themselves up; since not thus does the Gospel teach us.*' The correspondence between the two passages is marked. The conduct of Polycarp in waiting in order to be delivered up is in harmony with the Gospel; that of Quintus in hurrying to give *himself* up is not. The fanaticism of provoking persecution will meet us again in the African Church, where it produced serious disorders.

But the pattern set by Polycarp was not immediately needed at Smyrna. He was the last victim of this persecution. Popular fury was for the moment satiated, and the proconsul, who seems to have been at heart not hostile to the Christians, refused to make any further investigations respecting them. The date of this concluding martyrdom has been the subject of much controversy and most elaborate calculation. It has now been established as A.D. 155 or 156.

Both the martyr Polycarp and the apostate Quintus had their followers among subsequent bishops of Smyrna. Of these, Thraseas seems to have suffered martyrdom, while Eudæmon is said to have sacrificed during the Decian persecution, A.D. 250, about the time when Pionius was martyred. But during the remainder of our period Smyrna produced no bishop or teacher of great eminence. For such we must look to other Churches in Asia.

Polycarp's successors

Among those who followed close upon the age of the Apostles there is no one more intimately connected with Polycarp than Papias, bishop of *Hierapolis*. Our earliest informant couples them together. Papias, says Irenæus, was a 'hearer of John and a companion of Polycarp.' The first statement may be a mere inference from the second. Polycarp was John's disciple; Papias was Polycarp's companion; therefore Papias was John's disciple. But the inference, if it be one, has probability on its side. The last Apostle was living during the first thirty years of Papias; and what we know of Papias leads us to believe that he would not have failed to seek out St. John and converse with him. And it is possible that Irenæus is not drawing inferences, but stating a fact, of which he, as Polycarp's pupil, had personal knowledge. But

His companion Papias

the question thus cleared is again obscured by the fact that this John may after all be the hypothetical personage known as John the Elder, and not the last of the Apostles. Nevertheless the connexion between Polycarp and Papias remains undisturbed.

Hierapolis was a famous watering-place, whose name of 'sacred city' was justified by the profusion of temples with which it was adorned. Their magnificence is attested by the ruins which still remain. Here the Stoic slave Epictetus was learning his lofty pagan morality at the time when the far loftier doctrine was brought thither by Epaphras. When the destruction of Jerusalem caused Christians to migrate from Palestine, some of them settled at Hierapolis Among these were Philip the Apostle and his daughters, one of whom married and settled in Ephesus, while two others survived their father and lived to a great age in Hierapolis. From them Papias obtained various traditions of the Apostles and their contemporaries. He also obtained information from two disciples of the Lord, Aristion and John the Elder. It is on the interpretation of the passage in which he tells us this that the existence of a second John the Elder, distinct from the Apostle, depends. Papias collected traditions about Christ and the Apostles, and used them to illustrate the Gospel narrative in a treatise called 'An Exposition of the Oracles of the Lord,' some precious fragments of which are preserved by Eusebius. Eusebius had a low opinion of his intellectual power, and the fragments rather confirm this view; but Eusebius was prejudiced against him by his Millenarianism.

Papias has been put forward as one of those who

are supposed to have taken part in a revolt against the
teaching of St. Paul and a restoration of Judaism in Asia Minor. This revolt, headed, we
are told, by St. John and illustrated by Papias, is purely
imaginary. One of the chief arguments for the hypothesis is the alleged silence of Papias about the
teaching of St. Paul. But the argument breaks down
in two ways. (1) In the fragment in which Papias
speaks of collecting the sayings of Apostles and early
disciples, he is speaking of those who had heard Christ's
words; and among such St. Paul could not be included.
Moreover, there is nothing in St. Paul's writings that
would have helped Papias so materially in his work
that he would have been sure to quote it had he not
been prejudiced against him. (2) The alleged silence
of Papias is really the silence of Eusebius, who had
no reason to mention what use Papias made of St.
Paul. Polycarp and Irenæus are full of quotations from
St. Paul; and yet Eusebius, in stating their relation
to the Canonical Books, never mentions that they make
any use of St. Paul's Epistles. These Epistles were so
thoroughly attested and accepted, that it was unnecessary to mention who made use of them. We may say,
therefore, that the silence of Papias about St. Paul would
not prove antagonism, and that it is by no means certain
that he was silent about him. It is improbable that in
this matter Papias differed from his companion Polycarp;
and if he had differed very materially, Irenæus would
not have appealed to him as handing on the tradition
of the Apostles as to the teaching of Christ.

Papias not an Ebionite

The birth of Papias may be fixed A.D. 60–70, but
he was probably an elderly man when he wrote his

'Exposition.' False interpretations of the Gospel had already become numerous, and required to be counter-acted. We cannot, therefore, date the treatise much before A.D. 130. By this time the writings of the Gnostic leader Basilides were in circulation, and there is good reason for believing that it was the wild interpretations of Gnostics, and perhaps of Basilides in particular, that Papias desired to oppose. This agrees with the significant statement of Eusebius that Papias 'made use of testimonies from the First Epistle of John.' There is no better antidote to Gnosticism than St. John's First Epistle. We know from the quotations given by Hippolytus that Basilides seriously misinterpreted St. John's Gospel. How natural, therefore, that Papias should use the Apostle's own interpretation of his Gospel in order to refute the Gnostic! Papias also bears witness to the Gospels of St. Matthew and St. Mark, and tells us that 'Matthew composed the Oracles in the Hebrew language, and each one interpreted them as he could.' 'Interpreted,' not 'interprets': in the time of Papias the prevalence of the Greek Gospel of St. Matthew rendered interpretation of the Hebrew Gospel no longer necessary. There is good reason for believing that the paragraph about the woman taken in adultery, which certainly is no part of St. John's Gospel, is an authentic narrative from the traditions collected by Papias. The saying of Christ to the man found working on the Sabbath may come from the same source. 'Go thy way, from henceforth sin no more' would answer those Gnostics who contended that, the body being utterly evil, it mattered not how it was polluted; and 'O man, if thou knowest what thou doest, thou are blessed; but

<small>but an opponent of Gnosticism</small>

if thou knowest not, thou art accursed and a transgressor of the law,' would teach men that, though there is a higher way than the Law of Moses, yet the Old Testament is not the work of the evil one, nor are its precepts to be contemptuously disregarded.

Of the death of Papias we know nothing certain. The 'Chronicon Paschale' says that he suffered martyrdom at Pergamum at the same time as Polycarp suffered at Smyrna, and it places this in A.D. 163.

Among his neighbours was Abercius, Bishop of Hieropolis near Synnada. A life of him exists, written *Abercius of* probably c. A.D. 380, but it contains an *Hieropolis and his* epitaph, which was believed to be in the main *epitaph* authentic, and which has lately been to a large extent confirmed by a fragment of an epitaph found on a stone near Hieropolis, as well as by an adaptation of it on the tomb of a Christian named Alexander. Putting the three witnesses together, Bishop Lightfoot has reproduced the whole epitaph thus:—

'The citizen of a notable city I made this (tomb) in my lifetime, that in due season I might have here a resting place for my body. Abercius by name, I am a disciple of the pure Shepherd, who feedeth his flock of sheep on mountains and plains, who hath great eyes looking on all sides; for He taught me faithful writings. He also sent me to royal Rome to behold it and to see the golden-robed, golden-slippered Queen. And there I saw a people bearing the splendid seal. And I saw the plain of Syria and all the cities, even Nisibis, crossing over the Euphrates. And everywhere I had associates. In company with Paul I followed, while everywhere faith led the way, and set before me for food the fish from the fountain, mighty and stainless (whom a pure virgin grasped), and gave this to friends to eat always, having good wine and giving the mixed cup with bread. These words I, Abercius, standing by, ordered to be inscribed. In sooth I was in the course of my seventy-second year. Let every friend who observeth this pray for me. But no man shall place another tomb above mine. If otherwise, then he shall pay two thousand pieces of gold to the treasury of the Romans, and a thousand pieces of gold to my good fatherland Hieropolis.'

There are many points of interest here. The journeys to Rome and Euphrates are remarkable: and it was perhaps in Rome that he saw a representation of the Good Shepherd with large eyes watching his sheep on the mountains, probably in mosaic. Everywhere he finds fellow-Christians. The line containing the name Paul is uncertain; but it seems to mean that wherever he went he took St. Paul's writings with him; and, if so, it is further proof that in Phrygia there was no revolt against Pauline doctrine. Then follows what is perhaps the earliest allusion to the emblem of the fish (ΙΧΘΤΣ). The fountain is baptism, by which we are admitted to the Eucharist: and perhaps we have another reference to baptism in the people with the bright seal. The Queen and the pure virgin are not so clear; the former is possibly the Church in Rome, and the latter the Church universal.

Significance of the epitaph

Whether Abercius was a writer or not, we do not know. If he is the same as Avircius Marcellus, a treatise against Montanism, from which Eusebius quotes, was written at his request soon after the rise of that form of error. But at any rate the literary traditions of Phrygia were continued by the successor of Papias, Claudius Apollinaris. The patron deity of Hierapolis was Apollo, and if Claudius derived his name from the god, he was of pagan origin. The name was common in the district. Another form is Apolinarius. He was bishop of Hierapolis c. A.D. 170, and with Melito of Sardis was one of the most productive Christian writers of that age. He was conversant with heathen literature, and turned this knowledge to account in defending the faith. Eusebius and Photius give the titles of some of his works, and they cover a wide range of subjects both in and outside the sphere of Christianity. He wrote on Truth, on Piety, and on the Easter question. The fragments of the last work do not contain his views as to the main point, but there is no reasonable doubt that, like Polycarp, Melito, and Polycrates, he was a Quartadeciman. He wrote against the Encratites and also against those who denied the human nature of Christ. Like Abercius before him, he was much concerned about the spread of Montanism in Phrygia, although this form of fanaticism was then still in its first phase. Serapion of Antioch commended the treatise of Apollinaris on the subject, and Eusebius speaks of it as a 'strong and irresistible weapon' against the heresy. In this, which seems to have been one of his later writings, he anticipated Apollonius of Ephesus. That he called a Synod of twenty-six bishops, which excommunicated Montanus and Maximilla, rests on rather late authority, but is by no means improbable. Besides these works on Christian topics, he wrote a controversial treatise against the

Jews, another against the Gentiles, and addressed an Apology to the Emperor M. Aurelius. It was probably in this last that he alluded to the miracle of the Thundering Legion; and it must therefore have been written after A.D. 174. From him seems to have come the erroneous statement, which has thrown unnecessary doubt upon the whole story, that the *Legio Fulminata* took its name from the incident. The name was certainly in existence in the time of Nero, and probably of Augustus. It occurs under Nerva, Trajan, and Hadrian. The Apology is lost; and we are not quite certain that the allusion to the Thundering Legion was not in one of the other writings of Apollinaris. Jerome and Theodoret both speak in high praise of his writings, and Photius commends his style.

Apollinaris, bishop of Hierapolis, must be distinguished from two other persons; a presbyter of Alexandria, who like his namesake of Hierapolis was well versed in Greek literature, and who undertook to rewrite the Scriptures in a classical form; and a bishop of Laodicea, whose teaching was condemned at the Council of Chalcedon. Both these lived two centuries later than the defender of Christianity and opponent of Montanism: yet some confusion seems to exist in ancient writers, or in their readers. We pass on to another person even more distinguished.

In the latter half of the second century few persons were more prominent among the Christians of Asia Minor than Melito, bishop of *Sardis*. He was one of those 'great lights' to whose authority Polycrates of Ephesus appealed in his controversy with Victor of Rome about the time of celebrating

Easter; and his whole life, says Polycrates, was under the influence of the Holy Spirit. Melito, like Apollinaris, addressed an Apology to M. Aurelius c. A.D. 177; and it would appear from the list of nineteen treatises by Melito which Eusebius gives us, that the Apology was written among the last. Eusebius quotes from the Apology and from two other writings. In one of these extracts Melito speaks of 'the Books of the Old Testament,' and thus by emphatic and repeated mention of *old* Biblical literature implies that there was already in existence a *new* Biblical literature. Eusebius does not profess to tell us the names of all Melito's works, and from Anastasius Sinaita (c. A.D 680) we learn the titles of one or two more. These two or three and twenty titles are full of interest and give a great deal of information. They show, even more completely than in the case of Apollinaris, how active Christian thought was in the latter half of the second century, and on what kind of subjects it exercised itself. The variety is very great, and goes far to prove that there was a large amount of culture in the Church in Melito's day. He would hardly have written had there not been Christians capable of appreciating his dissertations. Others before him had written about Easter, about Prophets and Prophecy; but, so far as we know, he was the first to treat about the Church, the Lord's Day, and the Devil, and perhaps he was the first to expound the Apocalypse. All these works, which would have been of the utmost interest, together with others on the Nature of Man, the Soul and Body, the Obedience of the Senses to Faith, &c., are lost. In the face of the intellectual activity implied by these writings of Melito and Apollinaris, to whom we may add Miltiades, Modestus, Rhodon, and Musanus, it is difficult to see how any great change in the Creed of the Church could have been attempted without being exposed and controverted. And yet we are sometimes asked to believe that a mass of spurious literature completely revolutionised Christianity just about the time when all this literary activity was displayed.

Of Melito's life we know hardly anything. He was regarded as a prophet; but we do not know what that Melito's implied. He made a journey to Palestine in canon of the O. T. order to obtain information respecting the Jewish Canonical Books. Of these he gives a list in one of the fragments preserved by Eusebius. It is the earliest Christian list of the Jewish scriptures. Neither Esther nor Nehemiah is mentioned in it, but either or both may possibly be included under Ezra. From Polycrates we know that he was a Quartadeciman. Perhaps this fact has caused him to be classed as a Montanist; for the Montanists were Quartadecimans. He taught the Divinity of Christ very emphatically. A writer against Artemon quoted by Eusebius asks, 'Who is ignorant of the books of Irenæus and Melito and the rest which declare Christ to be God and man?' The writer is probably Hippolytus.

If his Apology was one of the latest of his writings, and if this was written A.D. 170-177, Melito must have Th influ- been born soon after the death of St. John. ence of his writings He must have known Polycarp, Papias, and Apollinaris, for the distances between Smyrna, Hierapolis, and Sardis are small. We may count him among those 'elders' of Asia to whom Irenæus so constantly

THE CHURCHES IN ASIA MINOR 53

appeals; and it has been thought that he may be the Ionian who was one of the first teachers of Clement of Alexandria. The estimation in which his writings were held is proved by the way in which they are quoted by leading Christians in very different parts of the Empire; by Polycrates at Ephesus, by Clement at Alexandria, by Tertullian at Carthage, by Hippolytus at Rome, by Origen in Alexandria and Palestine. Tertullian praised Melito's *elegans et declamatorium ingenium*, and the fragments of Melito which remain are evidence of a decidedly rhetorical style. He was one of the earliest Christian writers to look forward to a time when Christianity would become the official religion of the Empire. In this Justin Martyr to some extent anticipates him.

There is a remarkable fact about every one of the writers who illuminated the Churches in Asia Minor during the second century, which must not be passed over in silence. Polycarp, Papias, Apollinaris, Melito, and Polycrates, all of them, either directly or indirectly, supply evidence as to the recognition of the Fourth Gospel. Each item of evidence can be discredited on the hypothesis of forgery, or of interpolation, or of a spurious gospel somewhat similar to the Fourth. A separate hypothesis is required to explain away each one of the items of evidence. The *one* hypothesis which explains them *all* is, that the Fourth Gospel was in existence and was recognised as authentic.

[Marginal note: Asiatic evidence respecting the Fourth Gospel]

Notice of the Church in Bithynia is reserved for another chapter. Its history illustrates the sufferings rather than the energies of the early Christians.

CHAPTER V.

THE CHURCHES IN GREECE AND EGYPT.

Of the spread of Christianity in Greece during this period we have comparatively little evidence, but enough to show that the seed planted by St. Paul had taken deep root. The contest with the ancient faiths was, however, a long one. In this its old home Greek paganism died hard. It lingered on side by side with its conqueror into the Middle Ages.

The Church of *Athens* gives us several persons of note. From Dionysius of Corinth, quoted by Eusebius, we learn that Dionysius the Areopagite, one of the few converts won by St. Paul in this home of intellectual frivolity (Acts xvii. 34), was the first bishop of Athens. If this statement, written only a century later than the alleged fact, be rejected, then we must explain it as Renan does: 'Episcopacy had already become the form without which the existence of a Christian community seemed inconceivable.' The long believed and still defended theory, that the Areopagite was also the first Apostle of Gaul and the author of writings which since the sixth century have borne his name, is absolutely untenable. The silence of Eusebius would be very remarkable if either identification were correct. Gregory of Tours places the coming of St. Denys into France in the third century (c. A.D. 250); and the theological phraseology of the writings is that of a later age still, and can hardly be earlier than the fifth.

THE CHURCHES IN GREECE AND EGYPT 55

Publius, the successor of the Areopagite at Athens, was martyred under Antoninus Pius (A.D. 138-161). Jerome places the martyrdom in the reign of Hadrian (A.D. 117-138), but in this he is probably drawing a wrong inference from his sole authority Eusebius, who knows nothing of a persecution under Hadrian and gives no date to the martyrdom of Publius.

Quadratus succeeded Publius as bishop of Athens; and by his exertions the community which had been dispersed by the persecution was once more brought together and encouraged. Jerome identifies him with the earliest known Apologist, who addressed an Apology to Hadrian (c. A.D. 126), and hence infers that it was under Hadrian that his predecessor suffered. But we probably have two, if not three, persons of the name of Quadratus in Eusebius: the Bishop of Athens (IV. xxiii. 3); the Apologist (IV. iii. 1, 2); and the Prophet (III. xxvii. 1 ; V. xvii. 2, 4). The first two are connected with Athens, the third not.

About the same time as Quadratus, or perhaps a few years later, another Athenian Christian, Aristides, presented an Apology for the faith to Hadrian. Jerome says that he was a philosopher of great eloquence, and that his treatise was still extant and esteemed by scholars. That Aristides pleaded before the Emperor in person is a later addition and improbable.

Aristides the Apologist

Some fifty years later Athens gave to the Church another defender of the faith in Athenagoras. He also was a philosopher, as he himself tells us, and two of his works are still extant. The Πρεσβεία περὶ Χριστιανῶν, or 'Embassy about Christians,' i.e. Plea on behalf of Christians, is addressed to the

Athenagoras the Apologist

Emperors Aurelius, Antoninus, and Commodus. It answers the vulgar charges of atheism, cannibalism, and incest by an appeal to the rites and lives of Christians, and by contrasting those of their heathen accusers. The genuineness of the treatise 'On the Resurrection of the Dead' has been doubted on insufficient grounds. In it he endeavours to reconcile the Greek mind to the doctrine of the Resurrection by arguments drawn from the destiny of man and the attributes of God. Both works are held in high estimation for style as well as for power. They seem to have been unknown to Eusebius. Neither he nor Jerome mentions Athenagoras.

It is probable that Epiphanius is correct in stating that Clement of Alexandria was an Athenian by birth. But, even if this were a certainty, it would be misleading to treat of him as belonging to his birthplace rather than to the city in which his great work was done. It is possible that Athenagoras was one of his early instructors.

The history of the Athenian Church during the third century is a blank.

Another important witness as to the condition of Christianity in Greece is found at *Corinth*. What the Church of Corinth was at the close of the first century we learn to some extent from the Epistle addressed to it by the Church of Rome through its bishop, Clement. It is a unique document of the sub-Apostolic age, and a priceless monument of the primitive Church. It may possibly be older than portions of the New Testament, and almost certainly was written before the death of St. John. It is written in a parental tone to deplore the feuds which have again

[margin: Epistle of Clement to the Corinthians]

THE CHURCHES IN GREECE AND EGYPT 57

broken out in the Corinthian Church after having been healed by the teaching of St. Paul. Envy, which has wought such mischief in the world, is their besetting sin. Harmony rules wherever God is truly Lord: why not in their hearts also? Hearts must be cleansed, for He reads them. All impurity, contention, and pride must be rooted out. Differences of rank and office are necessary; in the Church, as in the world. They do wrongly, therefore, who rebel against presbyters, who have been duly appointed and have proved faithful ministers. Let those who began this dispute begin the repentance.

All this shows that the characteristic faults of the Corinthian Church, though checked, were not extinct.

Its significance And it also shows with what affectionate frankness one Church ventured to exhort and reprove another. For the letter is from ' the Church of God which sojourneth in Rome to the Church of God which sojourneth in Corinth.' It is not a pastoral from the Bishop of Rome. Neither is Clement's name mentioned, nor is his episcopal office indicated, throughout the whole letter. The community, not its overseer, speaks —always in the first person plural. 'We consider;' 'we write;' 'we mean;' 'receive our counsel;' 'joy and rejoicing will be put in our hearts if ye will hearken to what we have written in the Holy Spirit;' 'we have sent men who will be witnesses betwixt you and us;' 'send back our messengers speedily... that we also may the more speedily rejoice;' 'our whole care both was and is that ye should right soon have peace once more.' No legal right to control or rebuke another Church is claimed or insinuated. The moral right to use such language had its basis on two facts. (1) The Church of Corinth was weakened by dissension, while that of Rome was strong in peace and unity. (2) The Church of Rome was the Church of the world's metropolis, and as such felt its responsibilities to Christendom. We shall have to return to the subject of this letter again. No bishop of Corinth appears in it.

Another glimpse of the Church of Corinth is caught when Hegesippus 'spent many days' there on his way to Rome c. A.D. 160. Eusebius mentions Hegesippus with Melito, Apollinaris, and others among the contemporaries of M. Aurelius whose 'orthodoxy of sound faith derived from Apostolic tradition has come down in writing even to us.' He wrote five books of 'Jottings on Ecclesiastical Affairs,' of which we now have only a few fragments. He was a converted Jew; but it is an error to regard him as a Judaizing Christian. He approved the 'Epistle of Clement,' which is thoroughly Pauline in tone. He seems, like Papias, to have made his very miscellaneous collection of notes partly in order to refute Gnosticism. His main object was to show in opposition to heretics the purity and universality of Christian doctrine. Like Irenæus after him, he appealed to the preservation of the faith through the regular succession of bishops from the Apostles, and in particular he noticed the cases of the Churches of Corinth and of Rome. 'The Church of the Corinthians,' he says, 'remained in the right doctrine down to the episcopate of Primus in Corinth, with whom I had converse on my voyage to Rome: and I stayed with the Corinthians many days, in which we were mutually refreshed in the right doctrine.' The

Testimony of Hegesippus

meaning of the passage about Rome is a little uncertain, owing to a disputed reading. Hegesippus sums up thus: 'But in every succession and in every city there prevails just what the Law and the Prophets and the Lord proclaim.'

But the chief light of the Corinthian Church in our period is Dionysius, who probably succeeded Primus as bishop, and c. A.D. 170. His pastoral letters, which Eusebius speaks of as 'Catholic Epistles,' were held in such repute that heretics found it worth their while to tamper with them, just as (so Dionysius complains) 'they attempted to tamper with the Scriptures of the Lord.' Eusebius prefaces his notice of the writings of Dionysius thus : 'And first we must speak of Dionysius, that he was entrusted with the seat of the oversight (episcopal chair) of the Church in Corinth, and how he imparted liberally of his inspired industry, not only to those under him, but to those elsewhere also, making himself most useful to all in the Catholic Epistles which he indited to the Churches.' He wrote among others to the Churches of Lacedæmon, Athens, Nicomedia, Gortyna, and the other Churches in Crete, Amastris, and the Churches in Pontus, Cnossus, and Rome, as well as to his 'most faithful sister Chrysophora.' These letters, from which Eusebius gives some extracts, are evidence as to the prevalence of episcopacy at this time, and also as to the belief in its Apostolic origin. No less than seven bishops are mentioned : Dionysius the Areopagite, Publius, and Quadratus at Athens ; Philip and Pinytus in Crete, Palmas in Pontus, and Soter at Rome ; and the Areopagite is expressly connected with St. Paul. But, although Dionysius sometimes seems to have written in his own name, yet in writing to the Romans he states that he wrote because 'brethren begged me to write.' And in all cases he writes to the Church and not to the bishop. And that of Soter to him is spoken of as the letter of the Roman Church (ὑμῶν). He mentions that both this letter and the former one sent by Clement were read publicly in church at Corinth. It was probably owing to this practice that the homily commonly known as the 'Second Epistle of Clement' obtained its misleading name. It was kept along with the genuine Epistle for public use, and after a time they were spoken of as 'the two Epistles,' and then 'the two Epistles of Clement.' But it cannot be quoted as evidence of the Corinthian Church; for it is quite an open question whether it was originally intended for that Church. Its date and authorship are also quite uncertain; but we may place it before A.D. 150, and consider it as the earliest Christian sermon that has come down to us.

Near the end of the second century we find Bacchylus, bishop of Corinth, who may easily have been the immediate successor of Dionysius. He was prominent in the second phase of the Paschal controversy when Victor of Rome came into collision with Polycrates of Ephesus and the Asiatic Churches. Bacchylus wrote a letter, as did many other bishops, in favour of celebrating Easter always on the Lord's day. The *Liber Synodicus* states that he presided at a Council at Corinth on the question; but Eusebius says expressly that his letter was written in a private capacity (ἰδίως), and a Synod, had it met, would have made some official report. Jerome contradicts the ἰδίως by saying that

Bacchylus wrote in the name of all the bishops of Achaia —*ex omnium persona*. Be this as it may, with Bacchylus what is known of the Church of Corinth during the first three centuries ends. We pass on to consider another Christian centre which has had more influence upon the thought and literature of Christendom than any Church in Greece.

The Church of *Alexandria* is an attractive but bewildering subject for the student; the materials for its history are so interesting and so abundant, and lie in such various directions; and the influences at work in it and in contact with it are so many and so great. Its powers are manifest, and its productions brilliant; but their positive results it is by no means easy to comprehend or to weigh. For nearly a thousand years (B.C. 330 to A.D. 640) Alexandria stood at the head of the intellectual world. It gradually absorbed the wisdom and mental activity both of Greece and of the East, both of Paganism and Judaism. The intellectual vitality, which had been crushed elsewhere by the conquests of Alexander and their consequences, found a new home created for it in Egypt by the conqueror himself. His successors developed it. Under the Ptolemies Alexandria became possessed of far the largest and most complete library in the world, with scholars and philosophers to expound and increase its contents. The Gospel added another quickening impulse, the most powerful of all; and it rapidly precipitated the subtle elements, with which the intellectual atmosphere of Alexandria was charged, round itself as a new centre. Behind all this was the majestic background of ancient Egypt. There were tombs and monuments beside which even Moses himself was modern. The Alexandrian, who lived amidst the quickest pulsations of contemporary thought and life, was the heir of a history which was old when the Greek nation was born. Yet it was the restlessness rather than the repose of Alexandria that most impressed the visitor. 'No one,' says the Emperor Hadrian, 'lives there in idleness. The lame have their occupation; the blind follow a craft; even the crippled lead a busy life.' But the critical spirit of the place had marred its creative powers. It produced; but its productions were unsubstantial. Religion was evaporated in allegory; philosophy was lost in arbitrary and dreamy speculation. Not even Jewish beliefs had proved strong enough to resist the powerful solvents with which they there came in contact. Moses was explained away scarcely less freely than Plato in the attempt to reconcile both with prevailing currents of thought. 'What is Plato but Moses speaking in Attic?' And what is true of the Alexandrian School before it admitted Christianity remains to some extent true of it afterwards, especially during our period. It is suggestive rather than solid. Its errors are abundant, although instructive. And it is richer in influence than in tangible results.

And first to distinguish the various meanings of 'Alexandrian School.' Chronologically there are two

The Alexandrian Schools Alexandrian Schools. The first was concerned chiefly with literature, and its day was over before the Christian era. It almost perished when Alexandria became Roman, c. B.C. 30, and the Roman literature of the Augustan age is to a large extent its child. The second was concerned mainly with philosophy, and sprang from the contact between Greek and Jewish ideas. It produced Neo-Platonism and Gnosticism, both of which endeavoured to make terms with Christianity and powerfully influenced it. But in this second and philosophical period 'Alexandrian School' is used in more than one signification. Sometimes it is used to express certain tendencies or habits of thought in philosophy and theology. Sometimes it means the great Catechetical School, which from obscure beginnings became the chief intellectual institution in the Empire; and, under the hand of Clement, Origen, and their successors, assumed the proportions of a university. It is in connexion with this institution that the Church of Alexandria becomes such an important centre in the second and third centuries. The bishops of Alexandria were comparatively unimportant persons during this period.[1] It is the teachers in the Catechetical School who have exerted such a powerful and abiding influence over the Christian Church. At Alexandria, as in Palestine, the rabbi eclipsed the priest.

The origin of the school is not known. Christ Himself had ordered that the Apostles should 'make dis-

[1] The list of bishops during the first two centuries, with their approximate dates, is as follows: Annianus A.D. 63, Abilius 86, Cerdo 98, Primus 109, Justus 120, Eumenes 130, Marcus 143, Celadion 154, Agrippinus 168, Julian 180, Demetrius 190. The title πάπας is applied to Heraclas, the successor of Demetrius (233), by his successor Dionysius (Eus. *H E*. VII. vii. 4). Not until the sixth century did *papa* begin to be restricted to Roman bishops. This application of the title 'Pope' to Heraclas is perhaps connected with the increase of the Egyptian Episcopate. Down to A.D. 190 the bishops of Alexandria were the only bishops in Egypt. Demetrius added three others, and Heraclas twenty more.

ciples' before baptizing, and everywhere we find that instruction in the faith preceded admission to the Church. In a great intellectual centre such as Alexandria it was necessary that this instruction should be of a very high order. There the experience of the Apostle was not unfrequently reversed, and ' many wise ' and ' many mighty ' *were* called to the truth. The conversion of scholars and philosophers on the one hand and the spread of Gnostic errors on the other made it imperative to have minds of the keenest intellectual power and of the highest education to give systematic teaching both to catechumens and to the baptized. This need produced the Catechetical School at Alexandria. Instruction was given for the most part in private houses; but the lectures were public and gratuitous, and were often attended by Jews and heathen who had no intention of embracing Christianity. As the name indicates, the method was chiefly oral, and probably both teacher and taught propounded questions for discussion. It was under the superintendence of the bishop; and it was he who appointed the catechists or teachers. But it was not ecclesiastical. Its staff were not necessarily clergy. Like the Schools of the Prophets under the Law, it was largely independent of the hierarchy. Its object was partly to absorb, and partly to counteract, the intellectual influences outside Christianity.

We first find definite information about it when Pantænus becomes its chief teacher, a little before A.D. 180. Nicephorus Callistus (fourteenth century) quotes Philip of Sida (fifth century) as stating that Athenagoras was the first head of the school. Philip also makes Pantænus, like Athenagoras, an Athenian. Both statements lack confirmation; and the second seems to be contradicted by the passage about the last but best teacher of Clement in *Strom.* I. i. This almost certainly refers to Pantænus, and in it Clement calls him ' in truth a *Sicilian* bee, culling flowers from prophetic and apostolic meads, and engendering pure knowledge in the souls of hearers.' Eusebius praises the ability and learning of Pantænus, and speaks of the school as already ancient when he became its head. Jerome would trace its origin back to St. Mark; and Photius represents Pantænus himself as a hearer of the Apostles. This is scarcely possible; but he may well have been instructed in the faith by some who had themselves been taught by St. John. His own teaching was a continuation of Apostolic tradition put into a philosophic and scholarly form. Alexander, bishop of Jerusalem, writes of him as one of the fathers who had trodden the road before them, and as τὸν μακάριον ὡς ἀληθῶς καὶ κύριον. He went as a missionary as far as ' the Indians,' among whom he is said to have found in use the Hebrew Gospel of St. Matthew, believed to have been brought thither by St. Bartholomew. Jerome says that he was sent on this mission by Demetrius, who was bishop of Alexandria A.D. 189–233. If this is true, it was on his departure to the East that Clement succeeded him as head of the Catechetical School. But Eusebius seems to imply that Pantænus taught at Alexandria *after* his missionary work in the East. Of the many commentaries which he is said to have written nothing remains; and of all his writings only two fragments survive. They add very little to our knowledge of him. But any gleanings respecting Pantænus are of value; first, because with him the history of the Catechetical School (so far as it is known to us) begins; secondly, because from him the minds of his great successors, Clement and Origen, received instruction and impulse. It was he who set them the example of studying the opinions of heathen philosophers and heretics, in order to help such men to the truth. Moreover, in the very scanty information which we have of definite missionary work at this period, the account of his journey to 'the Indians' is of special interest, which is intensified by the reported discovery of the Hebrew Gospel of St. Matthew there. That he brought this document back to Alexandria, as Jerome asserts, is unlikely. Had he done so, Clement and Origen would have something more definite to tell us about it. But that he found any such document may be doubted: Eusebius gives it as a mere report or tradition (λόγος).

About his successor Clement (Titus Flavius Clemens) we have far more abundant information. Like Pantænus, who was originally a Stoic, he was led through philosophy to the truth. He tells us that he had studied in Greece, Italy, and the East, under teachers from Ionia, Cœlesyria, Assyria, and Palestine, before he found the last in order, 'but in power first,' Pantænus. There is good reason for believing that the Assyrian teacher here mentioned is Tatian; the Ionian may be Melito. Like Hegesippus and Irenæus, Clement appeals to the continuity of the doctrine which he has received. In a passage which is of great importance as illustrating the abundant intercourse between the Churches, and the agreement in their teaching in

Clement of Alexandria

Clement's time, he writes of his teachers thus : 'These men, preserving the true tradition of the blessed teaching directly from Peter and James, from John and Paul, the holy Apostles, son receiving it from father (but few are they who are like their fathers), came by God's providence even to us, to deposit among us those seeds which are ancestral and Apostolic.'

Clement was head of the Catechetical School from c. A.D. 190-202 or 203, when the persecution under Septimus Severus, in which the father of Origen suffered martyrdom, drove him from Alexandria. Eusebius does not state this distinctly, but he leaves us to infer it. The case is analogous to Cyprian's. That it was not mere timidity which caused each of them to retire is shown by their conduct afterwards. Clement visited his pupil Alexander, afterwards bishop of Jerusalem, during his long imprisonment, at the risk of being imprisoned himself; and Alexander, in sending him to congratulate the Church of Antioch on the succession of Asclepiades, writes of him in these high terms : ' This letter I send to you by Clement, the blessed presbyter, a man of virtue and tried merit, whom ye also know of and will learn to know still more, who by his presence here too, through the providence and guidance of the Ruler of all, has confirmed and increased the Church of the Lord.' Evidently Alexander saw nothing to criticise in Clement's departure from Alexandria. Nor did his successor Origen. This mission for his pupil is the last notice that we have of Clement (A.D. 211). Possibly he remained in Antioch. He seems never to have returned to Alexandria ; and the manner and date of his death are quite unknown.

He leaves Alexandria

Ten works of Clement's are known to us by name; and once more, as in the case of Apollinaris and Melito, we see over how wide a field Christian thought now ranged; and in Clement's case we have a better opportunity of judging with what power the various subjects were treated. Of the ten works mentioned by Eusebius, four have come down to us almost entire, with considerable fragments of a fifth, and a few fragments of three others. Most of those which have come down to us can be dated with some exactness. Their contents show that they were written in this order: 'The Address to the Greeks' first, for it is mentioned in 'The Tutor,' which in turn is mentioned in 'The Miscellanies;' and as the chronology of 'The Miscellanies' ends with the death of Commodus, we may place all three treatises between A.D. 190 and 200.

(1) The contents of the first of these three shows that it is addressed to *Greeks*, and not *Gentiles*, as Jerome translates "Ελληνας. The appeal throughout is to Greek religion and Greek philosophy, to both of which Christianity is shown to be superior in power and purity, in clearness and reality. The minute knowledge of heathen rites which this work displays shows that this Christian presbyter had been originally a pagan, and had possibly been initiated in some heathen mysteries.

(2) 'The Tutor' or 'Teacher' (c. A.D. 195) is described by Clement himself in 'The Miscellanies' as furnishing a system to prepare the souls of the young with virtue to fit them for the reception of the higher knowledge. Christ the Word is the Tutor, and all believers are the pupils, whom He trains by love and chastisements. Minute directions as to conduct are given; how to

bathe and to dress, what shoes to wear, what to eat and to drink, and the like, as well as more important counsel respecting education and the spiritual life. These directions give a vivid impression of the difficulties which confronted a Christian at every turn, as he mixed in the heathen society of that age. They show also the intensity with which Christianity was laying hold of every department of human life. And the frequent warnings against luxury and extravagance prove that the Church at this time included large numbers of wealthy people. The same fact is forced upon us by the contemporary writings of Tertullian. The work concludes with the oldest Christian hymn that has come down to us. It is probably not Clement's own composition, and may have been added by another writer. Some MSS. do not contain it. (3) 'The Miscellanies' is an unmethodical attempt to exhibit the capacities of the Gospel for satisfying the cravings and aspirations of man's nature. Its object is to suggest and excite rather than to teach. Out of these bundles of truths, half-truths, and errors, each is to pick what he needs for instruction and warning. In contrast to the heathen and heretical enquirer, the true Gnostic is sketched and the ideal of the Christian scholar and philosopher is put before us. (4) The remaining entire work is a simple discourse based on Mark x. 17–31 in answer to the question, *Who is the Rich Man that is in the way of salvation?* It is the source of the beautiful story of St. John and the Robber, so well known from the reproduction of it by Eusebius.

We must think of Clement as above all things a teacher, a professor or lecturer, rather than a writer.

He cares little about literary style. So long as he is understood, so long as he can suggest the right thoughts to his readers, he does not care whether the language which he uses is elegant or not, or whether his work has symmetry and finish. In his day the oral tradition of Christ's teaching had died out, and written deductions from the written New Testament were being formulated. He stands at the threshold of the new era and warns us that we must not rest in such deductions as adequate or final. They are structures, not in which the truth can be confined, but in which what has been gained may be secured, while we rise by means of them to something fuller, and higher, and nearer to the source of all truth. Christianity is the inheritor not merely of the Law and the Prophets, but of everything that is true and helpful in heathen philosophy. God's creatures have been groping after Him in the past; but that is only half the blessed fact. He also has been seeking, and is seeking, them. In the distorted speculations and even in the gross fables of heathenism He was leading them through perplexity and disgust to Himself. In the elements of truth which paganism possessed there was a proof that God had not left man in ignorance of his Master, and a pledge that He would reveal more to him hereafter. Thus Clement continues the work of Justin Martyr; but he carries it much farther. Justin knew Greek philosophy and took a liberal view of it. But Clement had a far wider acquaintance with the whole round of Greek literature. The names of the writers quoted by him fill fifteen columns in Migne. Unlike his contemporaries, Irenæus and Tertullian, instead of condemning Greek philosophy as untrue, and as an obstacle to the faith, he regards it rather as containing precious fragments of truth, and as a stepping-stone to the Gospel. The 'wisdom of the ancients was a part of God's plan in educating the world.' In this respect heathen philosophers, Jews, and heretics are alike; they are all of them in possession of a portion of the truth. This they received from the Divine Logos, and it ought to lead them back to Him. From the incarnate Word full knowledge comes. In Him, therefore, we must believe. From faith, through love, to knowledge; that is the progress of the true Gnostic.

It has been disputed whether Clement is Aristotelian, or Neo-Platonic, or eclectic. The doubt suggests the true answer. He is none of these. He adopts no system, but makes use of any to express and illustrate the truth. His mind is a commonplace-book full of all kinds of topics and all kinds of thoughts about them. These are often touched with masterly power, but he makes no attempt to round them off into a system either of philosophy or faith. His teaching, with all its loftiness of tone, liberality, and suggestiveness, has two serious faults: extravagant license in allegorising Scripture, and intellectual exclusiveness. The one error to a large extent involves the other. If everywhere in the Bible there is a mystical meaning hidden from the eyes of the vulgar, who see only the literal sense, then it follows that the Bible is a closed book, to which, not all Christians, but only a favoured few, have access. He reproduced the error of the Greek philosophers, and made truth unattainable by any but the initiated. This error in Clement had

His own philosophy and its defects

its root in reverence. He wished, on the one hand, to exalt the glories of the written Word, on the other to preserve these glories from being profaned by being made familiar. But this is a reverence which may easily foster spiritual pride and superstition. The philosophic Christian 'condescends' to the literal meaning of Scripture for the sake of the unlearned and ignorant. He puts a veil upon that which God has left open to all, and confines it to his own use. He substitutes his own ingenuity for the Divine simplicity, and treats God's Word as a magic spell, of which he alone knows the meaning. Clement's large-minded charity preserved him from these evils; but the tendency to them is present in his teaching. It was the mission of Christianity to dispel the figment of a philosophical elect, specially favoured by God on account of their intellectual enlightenment.

The glory of the Catechetical School and of the Church of Alexandria culminates in Origen, the greatest of the pupils of Clement. Of all the Greek theologians, he is the mightiest and the most widely influential. He is the father of scientific theology and of Biblical criticism; and those who condemned his teaching in the sixth century were far more his disciples than his refuters. It would be impossible to name any one—either among his followers or his opponents—who approached him in the power which he exhibited in promoting sacred learning, in reconciling philosophy and religion, in confuting and converting pagans, Jews, and heretics, and in proving that Christianity supplies the noblest ideals to both the intellect and the will of man. Even the hostile and untiring

Greatness of Origen in his writings

THE CHURCHES IN GREECE AND EGYPT 73

Jerome praises his imperishable genius, and declares that he would bear the odium which he and others had heaped upon Origen, if he could have his knowledge of the Scriptures.

But Origen's wide and enduring influence was not due simply to his pen. He taught unceasingly by word of mouth, and above all by his devoted, self-denying life. 'As his word, so was his conduct; and as his conduct, so was his word,' was the testimony of his disciples to the beautiful consistency between his teaching and his acts. Telling as his arguments were, his own conduct was more convincing than his reasoning. His life was an earnest striving after his own great ideal. It was 'one continuous prayer;' one unwearying search for closer union with the Infinite and the Divine; 'to become like to God, with a pure mind; to draw near to Him, and to abide in Him.' The details of his life are as interesting as a romance, and fully in harmony with the lofty tone of the portion of his writings which has come down to us. No more than an outline can be given here; but it may lead the reader to study it more in detail elsewhere.

and in his life

Origen was born c. A.D. 185, at the time when Pantænus was at his best, when Clement was attending his lectures, when Irenæus was just completing his great work against heresies, and when Tertullian was deciding to embrace Christianity. Before this time there must have been many who had been Christians from infancy; but in Origen we have the first account of the bringing up of a Christian child. His father Leonides gave him a liberal education, and

His boyhood

instructed him carefully in the Scriptures. This shows that the Bible was already a family book, and was not reserved for the study of the clergy. The lad was made to learn portions by heart, and amazed his father by the questions which he asked about them. These showed the bent of his mind. He could not rest content with the literal meaning, and wished to know what else the words meant. His father checked his curiosity, and told him to be satisfied with what he could understand; but when the boy was asleep he used to kiss his breast—as the temple of the Holy Spirit—and to thank God for giving him such a child. Thus the education of heart and mind went on side by side. Clement, and perhaps Pantænus, instructed him along with his father; and from them he derived the impulse, which afterwards produced such noble results, towards exhibiting the Gospel on an intellectual basis, and in a philosophic form.

In the persecution under Septimius Severus, Leonides was imprisoned. Origen would have shared his father's fate, but his mother hid his clothes. He wrote, however, to his father, to entreat him not to let any thought of the family induce him to change. This is the earliest writing of Origen's of which we have information, and it was known to Eusebius. Leonides was beheaded A.D. 202, and Origen with his mother and six younger children were left penniless. A rich lady received him into her house. But she had adopted a young heretical teacher, who used to lecture and hold prayer-meetings at her house. At the risk of being turned out of doors, Origen refused to attend these meetings, and protested against the doctrine taught at them. To secure independence, he sold his writings on profane subjects for an income of four obols, or about eightpence, a day; and on this he lived for years. When he was only eighteen, Demetrius made him head of the Catechetical School. Demetrius had been bishop for some fourteen years; a man of energy, but greatly inferior to Clement and Origen in ability. But, though unequal to giving general instruction himself, he knew the right man for the post, and Origen's youth did not deter him from appointing him, 'there being no one at Alexandria,' says Eusebius, 'who devoted himself to teaching, but all having been driven away by the threatening prospect of the persecution;' which can only mean that Clement had fled and left the post empty. Origen in his later works is far from condemning such retirement. He says that no rule can be laid down: everything depends upon the circumstances and the call. It is right neither always to avoid danger nor always to meet it. It needs the wisdom of a Christian philosopher to decide when he should withdraw himself and when he should stand fast. Temptation, when it comes unprovoked, must be endured with fortitude; but it is foolhardy not to avoid it when we may. In this persecution Origen became notorious for the enthusiasm with which he ministered to martyrs both before and during their trial, and even when on the road to death. Seven of his own catechumens won the martyr's crown. Yet in all this zeal he took what precautions were possible, and hid when he was pursued. Once he was caught, carried to the temple of Serapis, and told to distribute palm-branches to the worshippers. He did so, saying, 'Receive not the idol's palm, but the palm of Christ.' His courage and adroitness probably delighted the mob, who might easily have been infuriated at such defiance, and have torn him in pieces.

While teaching others he continued his own studies, especially in Hebrew, and attended the lectures of the philosopher Ammonius Saccas, the master of Plotinus.

Industry, Porphyry, who as a young man had known Origen, cavils at him for his devotion to heathen philosophy. Origen replies that, in dealing with the heretics and philosophic heathen who came to converse with him, it was quite necessary to study their opinions and writings, as Pantænus had done before him with so much benefit to others. It was a wise economy, as he says in a letter to Gregory, to use the borrowed jewels of Egypt to adorn the sanctuary of God. But it is a mistake to suppose with Jerome and Photius that Origen's second name, Adamantius, was given him to express either his endurance in work or his invincibility in argument; or, with Epiphanius, that he assumed it himself in vanity. The name was fairly common, and in his case was original. Origen comes from Orus, an Egyptian deity, as Dionysius from Dionysus. Christians did not avoid these pagan names. As a Christian adaptation of what was heathen in origin, it symbolises the bearer's own attitude towards the old faiths. In them there was much that could be put to innocent and useful purposes. During all this severe work he led a most hard life, and in a fit of *and indis-* misdirected zeal he acted on a literal inter-*creet zeal* pretation of Matt. xix. 12. That Origen, who afterwards went to such extremes in mystical interpretations, should have taken such a text literally is surprising. Perhaps it is evidence that his father's influence, urging him to be content with the literal meaning of Scripture, was still dominant. The spirit of Clement and the bias of Origen's own mind had not yet got the upper hand. We feel a similar surprise when we find Origen taking 'the acceptable year of the Lord' as a period of twelve months. His rash act of ascetism, though a civil offence as well as an ecclesiastical error, was condoned at the time by Demetrius and others, but it afterwards caused him serious trouble. In later life he condemns it himself: 'We who once conceived of God's Christ and God's Word after the flesh and after the letter, now are coming to know Him so no more.' In commenting on the text he warns his readers against taking it literally. Perhaps the lifelong conviction that he had made a fatal mistake in accepting the letter of Scripture in this case helped to drive him to extremes in preferring mystical interpretations afterwards.

During the pontificate of Zephyrinus he visited Rome, c. A.D. 213, or a little later. He tells us that he Visits to 'had a longing to see the very ancient Church Rome, Arabia, and of the Romans.' Possibly Hippolytus had Palestine invited him in order to gain his support in his controversy with Callistus; and certainly the intercourse with Hippolytus, who was leading the way in interpreting the Old Testament in detail, would add much to the interest of Origen's visit. Hippolytus thinks it worth while to mention in a homily that Origen was present when it was delivered. He was anxious to claim the sympathy of this young, but already famous, theologian; and it is probable that he had it. Origen was also sent to Arabia at the urgent request of the governor, who wished to consult him. Heraclas, one of his first converts and pupils, and like himself a hearer of Ammonius Saccas, helped him in teaching in the Catechetical School, and probably took charge of it during these absences. The fame of Heraclas for philosophical knowledge was such as to bring Julius Africanus from Palestine to hear him. A still longer absence soon followed. From c. A.D. 215 to 219 Origen was away from home. Political tumults in connexion with the massacre ordered by Caracalla seem to have driven him from Egypt, and he retired to Cæsarea in Palestine. Here his friend Alexander of Jerusalem and Theoctistus of Cæsarea made use of him to expound Scripture before them in the public services of the Church. His own Bishop Demetrius expostulated and protested against allowing a layman to preach when bishops were present. The two Eastern bishops defended their conduct by precedents. Whereupon Demetrius called Origen back to Alexandria.

The recall was the beginning of that 'double martyrdom' of which his life is so marked an example. He had suffered, and was to suffer again, perils and persecutions from the heathen; but his chief trial was the captious hostility of fellow-Christians. He had the misfortune at the outset to be under the control of a man who was immensely his inferior in character and in ability. But the return to Alexandria had another side. It was now that Ambrosius, whom Origen had converted from Gnosticism, began to exercise his beneficial influence on his teacher, who playfully called him his 'taskmaster.' It is to the importunity of this Ambrose that we owe the commentary on St. John and most of Origen's exegetical works, as well as the treatise against Celsus, written later at Cæsarea. Short-

Influence of Ambrose

hand writers (ταχυγράφοι) took down Origen's words, and then scribes copied out the notes. Origen warns Ambrose that he is violating the advice of Solomon to avoid 'making many books.'

The success and celebrity of Origen was too much, Eusebius tells us, for the human sensibility of Demetrius; and he now turned against him. Origen unhappily gave him an opening. An invitation from Greece afforded Origen an opportunity for again leaving home, and on his way he was ordained presbyter at Cæsarea 'at the hands of the bishops there.' Demetrius may have been wrong before, but here he had just ground for complaint. His catechist had been ordained without his consent, and possibly against his wishes. Moreover, according to the first Nicene Canon, Origen's own rash act in early life would have been a bar to ordination; and there is good reason for believing that the rule is older than the Council of Nicæa, for Justin Martyr tells us that the question had arisen at Alexandria eighty years before Origen's case. On his return home Origen found that it was impossible for him to remain; and in 231 he left Alexandria never to re-enter it. It was Newman leaving Oxford; a noble son leaving a harsh parent, with a breaking heart, but without one angry word. Demetrius excommunicated him; but whether for insubordination or on a charge of heterodoxy is uncertain. Origen protested with dignity and moderation, as his enemies' own quotations show; and the sentence was entirely disregarded by the bishops of Palestine, Phœnicia, Arabia, and Greece. Demetrius was supported by Rome, and his successor Heraclas seems to have

Ordination and final departure from Alexandria

made no attempt to recall his former master and colleague.

Of Origen's twenty years of work at Cæsarea notice has already been taken in the account of that Church (pp. 26, 27). Of his manner of teaching in Palestine we have an enthusiastic account in the 'Panegyric' of Gregory Thaumaturgus, at this time one of Origen's pupils, and afterwards bishop of Neo-Cæsarea. Gregory says that no sooner had he and his brother come within the magic influence of Origen than they were caught like birds in a net, and could neither get on to Berytus, where they had intended to study law, nor home to Neo-Cæsarea. The great teacher held them spellbound. By a kind of divine power he fairly carried them away. He urged them to study philosophy; it was no true piety to despise this gift of God. He instructed them in natural science; the universe was to be contemplated with rational admiration, not with unreasoning amazement. Above all, he taught them to know themselves; without that knowledge all else was of little avail. Dialectic, physics, ethics; that was the *trivium* by which he trained them for the crowning science of theology. From only one class of literature did he warn them off; the advantage of knowing atheistic philosophy was not worth the risk of it. Everything else he encouraged them to master. Gregory sums up the charm of such a teacher in one word: 'He was truly a *paradise* to us.' And when at last he had to tear himself away from Cæsarea, he felt like Adam driven out of Eden. From 231 to 250 is the time of Origen's maturity, and most of his best work was done then. It suffered three interruptions. The persecution under Maximin the Thracian (235-237), in which his 'taskmaster' Ambrosius suffered, caused Origen to take refuge with Firmilian at Cappadocia in Cæsarea. And twice he was summoned to Arabia to argue with some who were teaching strange doctrine. In both cases he won over to the truth those who had gone astray. In this period (c. 238) falls his famous correspondence with Julius Africanus about the authenticity of the story of Susannah. He corresponded also with the Emperor Philip and his wife Severa. This helped to bring on him the wrath of Decius; but his eminence as a Christian teacher would have made him a victim in any case. Alexander of Jerusalem, Babylas of Antioch, and Origen were all imprisoned. The two former died. Origen was cruelly tortured, threatened, and kept in excruciating confinement; but he survived until the death of Decius brought about his release in 252. It was probably at this time that his old pupil Dionysius, now bishop of Alexandria, wrote to him 'On Martyrdom'; and in this it is pleasing to find the sternness of the Alexandrian Church towards its greatest son at last relaxing. His sufferings no doubt shortened his life. He died a little later (253 or 254) at Tyre, in the seventieth year of his age. His tomb was held in high honour until the Saracens destroyed Tyre in 1291.

Martyrdom and death

Three characteristics stand out conspicuous in Origen: the noble simplicity and unruffled calm of his life, often in the midst of the most irritating surroundings; his intense interest in intellectual pursuits, especially in whatever could throw light on revealed religion; and his enthusiasm in imparting

Characteristics

knowledge to others respecting the word and the works of God.

Like Clement, he is a teacher in an age of transition: but the transforming forces of the age are centred in him. No system of theology, in the modern sense of the term, is to be found in him; but great ideas, which have formed the materials of many systems, and great aspirations, which have given life to them. His philosophy is a hope and an ideal, rather than a system; and in working it out he is all things by turns—orthodox, Neo-Platonic, Gnostic, and critical. He furnishes his enemies with weapons for attacking him keener than they could themselves have forged, and sometimes he furnishes the enemies of the faith with such. But, in spite of serious errors here and there, he has 'laid down the true lines on which the Christian apologist must defend the faith against Polytheism, Judaism, Gnosticism, Materialism. These forms of opinion without the Church and within it were living powers of threatening proportions in his age, and he vindicated the Gospel against them as the one absolute revelation, prepared through the discipline of Israel, historical in its form, spiritual in its destiny.'

Services to Christianity

Origen was the author of great writings and great deeds; but he himself is greater than both. We feel it as we study his writings and read his life. He gave his disciples, he gives them still, not learning, not opinions, not rules, not advice, but himself. It is his own large heart and mind, his love of all truth, his yearning after the Divine, that he has communicated to Christendom.

His errors have two main sources. He is wanting in

historic feeling; and he attempts to solve the insoluble.
(1) The plain historical meaning of Scripture is sometimes arbitrarily set aside in order to make way
for an interpretation which is called mystical
and spiritual, in a way that leaves it open to the interpreter to make the text mean anything he pleases. The
meaning is read into the words, instead of being extracted from them. Like his teacher Clement, this
great master of Biblical interpretation too often reduced
exegesis to ingenuity in manufacturing riddles. (2)
Speculations as to the eternity of matter, the pre-exist-
ence of souls, the possibility of sin in a previous state,
the nature of the general resurrection, the extension of
redemption to the inhabitants of other planets, the con-
tinuance of an endless succession of worlds, the final
restitution of all, and even of Satan himself—all these are
problems which perhaps will never cease to be discussed,
but to which the human mind in this world is not likely
to find the answer. The discussion of them is not very
fruitful, and may easily become dangerous.

Sources of his errors

But there are questions more impertinent than
these, and among such is the enquiry as to Origen's
ultimate salvation, a subject sometimes formally discussed in the schools. Origen, we are
told, was condemned as a heretic; and can a heretic be
saved? But, as Dr. Newman urged more than fifty
years ago, 'that man of strong heart, who has paid for
the unbridled freedom of his speculations by the multitude of grievous and unfair charges which burden his
name with posterity, protests, by the forcible argument of
a life devoted to God's service, against his alleged connexion with the cold disputatious spirit, and the un-

Origen no heretic

principled domineering ambition, which are the historical badges of the heretical party.' Socrates, in the fifth century, gives us his explanation of the outcry against Origen, which in his day had already begun. Men of small ability, who had no chance of becoming distinguished by their own talents, tried to win themselves a name by abusing their betters. But 'those who revile Origen forget that they are calumniating Athanasius, who praised him.' He tells us of a Scythian bishop who refused to join in condemning Origen's writings, saying that he did not choose to outrage a man who had long ago fallen asleep in honour. There are few sadder chapters in Church history than those which contain the controversies about Origen. Happily they lie outside the scope of this volume. But to Origen himself we shall have to return later on, in connexion with the other master mind, to whom he forms so great a contrast—Tertullian.

One other great name distinguishes the Alexandrian Church at this period—Dionysius, sometimes called ὁ μέγας. He is perhaps the chief of the pupils of Origen. When Heraclas, Origen's colleague and successor, was promoted to the episcopate, Dionysius succeeded him as head of the Catechetical Schoool, A.D. 233; and, so far as we know, he retained the position, even after he himself became bishop, c. A.D. 247. He was banished in the Valerian persecution (257); but returned on the succession of Gallienus, who made Christianity practically, if not formally, a *religio licita*, A.D. 261.

Dionysius wrote much, but only fragments of his writings remain. The most important are the fragments of his letters, which Eusebius has incorporated in the sixth and seventh books of his History. Of these none is more interesting than the masterly criticism of the style of the Apocalypse in VII. xxv.

His letters

Like his master he attacked millenarian views; and he wrote against Sabellius. But he had also to defend his own orthodoxy against charges of the opposite error of making three Gods, and of regarding the Son as a creature or 'product' (ποίημα) of the Father. His namesake of Rome wrote to enquire as to this alleged error. The fragments of the Alexandrine's reply are doubly interesting. (1) They exhibit absolute independence: there is no evidence that either the one side claimed, or the other side admitted, any metropolitan or dogmatic authority as belonging to the see of Rome. (2) They indicate the dangerous ambiguity of the term *hypostasis*, which for the Roman expressed the Divine Nature, for the Alexandrine a Divine Person. It is not quite clear whether the Alexandrine wrote a separate letter to his namesake or merely sent him the four Books of his Defence against his Egyptian accusers (βιβλία ἐλέγχους καὶ ἀπολογίας).

His defence of himself

In taking part in the controversies of the time, Dionysius of Alexandria seems always to have been on the side of moderation. On the question of rebaptism he took the more liberal view against Cyprian, and on that of the lapsed, the more gentle view against the Novatians. In writing to Philemon, a presbyter of Rome, he relates how he was accustomed to read heretical books, being willing to

His moderation

acquaint his mind with error in order to refute and detest it more strongly. A presbyter warned him of the danger of becoming perverted: but in a vision a voice came to him telling him to read all that came to his hand, for he was qualified to prove all, and this very thing had helped his faith from the beginning. In combating the gross millenarian views of Nepos, an Egyptian bishop, he speaks with love and admiration of Nepos himself; and he conducted the controversy with the adherents of Nepos in a tolerant and conciliatory spirit. In dealing with Paul of Samosata he seems to have thought that it was still possible to win him back by argument. This was the last great question in which he took part. He was too infirm to attend the Council of Antioch in 265, and died that same year. His last years were much distracted by external troubles, of which he gives a vivid picture in a Paschal letter, A.D. 263. War, famine, and pestilence were the surroundings of the Easter festival. He contrasts the humanity of the Christians to the sick and dead with the selfish heartlessness of the heathen.

He was succeeded by Maximus, who with three other presbyters secretly shepherded the brethen in Alexandria when Dionysius was forced by the Christians of Mareotis to take refuge elsewhere from the Decian persecution. In the Valerian persecution he shared the banishment of the bishop. He held the see until A.D. 282, and was succeeded by Theonas. Peter followed in 301, Achillas in 312, and Alexander in 313. Achillas, like Heraclas and Dionysius, was head of the Catechetical School before being raised to the episcopate. He became bishop when Peter suffered

His successors

THE CHURCHES IN GREECE AND EGYPT 87

martyrdom in the last persecution. Arius the heresiarch was ordained deacon by Peter and presbyter by Achillas. Alexander is said to have put a stop to the alleged highly exceptional custom in the Alexandrian Church, according to which the presbyters not only appointed but ordained their bishop. This custom, if it really prevailed, may have arisen out of necessity. When the bishop of Alexandria was the only one in all Egypt, the presbyters would be driven to ordain or wait a serious time for a new bishop.

Alexandria naturally became a centre whence the Gospel spread to other parts. It was probably from Alexandria that Cyrene received the Gospel; for, of course, Mark xv. 21 does not imply that there were Christians in Cyrene when St. Mark wrote. The spread of the Gospel into Middle and Upper Egypt would be more difficult. So far as we know, there were there neither Jews nor Greeks to prepare the way and facilitate communication. Yet Eusebius tells us of a persecution of Christians in the Thebaid under Alexander Severus; and the Thebaic or Sahidic Version of the New Testament is probably as old as the third century.

Conversion of Middle and Upper Egypt

CHAPTER VI.
THE CHURCHES IN ITALY.

HITHERTO we have been considering the spread of Christianity among nations which were either Greek in origin or had received Greek elements through the conquests of Alexander. It was among them, as we might expect, that its chief and most rapid conquests were made. Its credentials were written in Greek, and Greek-speaking Jews were its first preachers. The early Christian writings which have come under our notice—the Epistles of Ignatius, Polycarp, and Dionysius, the Apologies of Justin Martyr, Athenagoras, and Theophilus, and the treatises of Papias, Clement, and Origen—were written in Greek. The questions of which they treat—the origin of the universe and of evil, the nature of God and His relations to mankind, are Greek also. The constitution of each Church exhibits the autonomy so dear to the Greek citizen; one in creed, in ministry, and in sacred rites with other Churches, and in closest fellowship with them; but forming an independent congregation under its own officers, and owing no obedience to the officers of other communities. The most ancient Churches took pride in their Apostolic origin and were reverenced on account of it; but as yet no supremacy of one Church over another was either admitted or claimed. The Greek-speaking half of the Roman Empire had no official centre, and Greek-speaking Christendom had no official centre either.

Early Christianity, Greek and uncentralised

We move in a new atmosphere when we pass on to watch the progress of the Gospel during the second and third century among those nations which for the most part spoke or understood the Imperial language of Rome. But even here, until the third century, all but the surroundings are to a large extent still Greek. And in literature even the surroundings are as much Greek as Latin. A Roman emperor writes his 'Meditations' in Greek; for Greek rather than

Roman Christianity Greek in origin

Latin is the language of all the world. The first Christian literature in Rome is Greek also. The Epistle of Clement, the 'Shepherd' of Hermas, the 'Clementine Homilies' and 'Recognitions,' and the writings of Irenæus and Hippolytus are all in Greek. The earliest Roman liturgy was in Greek, of which fact a trace still survives in the 'Kyrie Eleison.' At what date Rome acquired a Latin liturgy is quite uncertain. No extant Christian literature in Latin is older than A.D. 150; and, excepting Minucius Felix and the earlier works of Tertullian, there is very little of Latin Christianity that is older than the third century. Not until quite the end of the second (A.D. 189-199) do we find in Victor a Latin bishop of Rome. Eusebius mentions it as something remarkable that Cyprian and the African bishops wrote to Fabius of Antioch in Latin; Cornelius, bishop of Rome, wrote in Greek. But when Athanasius was in Rome, ninety years after this, he had to learn Latin, in order to instruct Bishop Julius and the Roman clergy as to what was really at stake (A.D. 340-343).

At the opening of the second century the Church of Rome had just sent its letters of rebuke and exhortation to the Church of Corinth. We need not doubt that the letter was written by Clement, whose name it commonly bears. But at the very outset it is stated that the sender is 'the Church of God which sojourneth in Rome.' The bishop of Rome is not mentioned, and St. Peter is not mentioned. No official person appears, and no supreme office is even named. The community, not an official, speaks throughout. That Rome should write rather than any other Church, is explained by the facts that Rome was the Empire's

Epistle of Clement

metropolis, whose Church had unique opportunities and obligations, and that through the intercourse between Rome and Corinth the Roman community would be specially conversant with the disturbed condition of the Corinthian Church. It is quite true that the intercourse between Ephesus and Corinth was great also, and that St. John was probably still living when this letter was written. But, at any rate, he must have reached that stage when he had to be carried to church, and could give no longer exhortation than 'Little children, love one another;' and the Church of Ephesus was not the Church of the metropolis. That the letter was not regarded at Rome as in any sense official is shown by the fact that it was precisely at Rome that its very existence was forgotten; whereas in the East it sometimes found a place in the Canon of the New Testament, and was publicly read in churches.

Our next clear view of the Church in Rome is in the Ignatian Epistles. Of the seven genuine letters the six which are addressed to communities in Asia are full of the duty of obeying their bishops; the letter to Rome has nothing of the kind. It styles the Church 'beloved and enlightened . . . worthy of honour, of felicitation, of praise, of success.' It implies that some of its members are powerful enough to obtain a pardon for Ignatius, and begs them not to try. But it contains no evidence that Rome has a bishop. 'To ourselves,' says Bishop Lightfoot, 'the Church of Rome has been so entirely merged in the bishop of Rome, that this silence is the more surprising. Yet, startling as this omission is, it entirely accords with the information derived from other trustworthy sources.

Epistle of Ignatius to the Romans

All the ancient notices point to the mature development of episcopacy in Asia Minor at this time. On the other hand, all the earliest notices of the Church in Rome point in the opposite direction. In the Epistle of Clement, which was written a few years before these Ignatian letters purport to be penned, there is no mention of the bishop. . . . The next document emanating from the Roman Church after the assumed date of the Ignatian Epistles is the " Shepherd " of Hermas. Here again we are met with similar phenomena. If we had no other information, we should be at a loss to say what was the form of Church government at Rome when the "Shepherd" was written.' At Rome the bishop in his relation to the presbyters is still only *primus inter pares*; the constitution of the Church is not monarchical, but collegiate.

Our next witness is the first Christian historian, the Jewish convert Hegesippus, who came from Palestine through Corinth to Rome in the episcopate of Anicetus (between A.D. 150 and 168). Polycarp, Justin Martyr, and Irenæus were in Rome about the same time. Like Irenæus after him, Hegesippus endeavoured to make a stand against the alarming growth of heresies; and the two writers use a similar argument. They quote the continuity of the episcopate as a guarantee for the permanence of Christian doctrine. Wherever he went in his travels Hegesippus found the same doctrine handed down. While in Rome he made out a list of the Roman bishops down to Anicetus in order to prove this continuity; and Irenæus has done the same. Unfortunately the list made by Hegesippus is not contained in the extant fragments of his work. The friendly dis-

Visits of Hegesippus and Polycarp to Rome

cussion between Anicetus and Polycarp as to the right day for celebrating Easter has been already mentioned (p. 40). No attempt was made on either side to coerce. Each agreed to hold to the tradition of his own Church.

Justin Martyr was twice in Rome. He contended there with the heretic Marcion, and his First Apology may have been written there c. A.D. 140. And he was martyred there c. A.D. 163. But his writings throw little light on the Roman Church. There is reason for believing that in his notices of the Eucharist he has the Church of Antioch in his mind; therefore we must not consider the 'President' ($\pi\rho o\epsilon\sigma\tau\grave{\omega}\varsigma$ $\tau\hat{\omega}\nu$ $\grave{a}\delta\epsilon\lambda\phi\hat{\omega}\nu$) as a reference to the bishop of Rome. It was probably the contest with heresy which hastened the development of episcopacy in the Roman Church. Cerdon, Marcion, Valentinus, and others had made Rome their headquarters; and in dealing with such leaders the need of having a head with recognised authority would be felt. The lapse of Florinus, the disciple of Polycarp, into one form of Gnosticism, and of Tatian, the disciple of Justin, into another, shows how full of danger the situation was. Florinus was a Roman presbyter, and Tatian had been a prominent teacher in Rome. We may date Roman episcopacy in the full sense of the term from the middle of the second century.[1] Certainly there can be no mistake about its development at the close of the century in the first Latin bishop, the imperious Victor.

The chronology of the Roman bishops during the

[1] Down to Anicetus Eusebius calls Roman bishops $\pi\rho\epsilon\sigma\beta\acute{\nu}\tau\epsilon\rho o\iota$. V. xxiv. 14.

Episcopacy in Rome promoted by heresy

THE CHURCHES IN ITALY 93

first two centuries is very uncertain; and for the most part their lives are very obscure. Some writers would have us believe that all of them were martyrs, together with all in the third century, excepting Dionysius and Eusebius. The post was no doubt one of danger, and hence the occasional vacancies; for to be overseer of the Christians there was to be a marked man, and in times of persecution the bishop would be the first to be attacked. Yet the first bishop of Rome of whose martyrdom we have historical evidence is Telesphorus, c. A.D. 138. And we have to pass over another century before we find another undoubted instance of martyrdom among the Roman bishops. Pontianus was exiled to Sardinia under Maximin, and died in exile, A.D. 235; and Fabianus was one of the first victims of the Decian persecution, January, 250.

Martyrs among the bishops of Rome

The correspondence between the Churches of Rome and Corinth during the episcopates of Soter and Dionysius has been already mentioned (see p. 60). The Roman letter is lost; but we gather from a fragment of the Corinthian answer that, like the Epistle of Clement, it was from the Church of Rome rather than from the bishop of Rome. Dionysius uses the plural throughout: ὑμῖν, πέμπετε, ὁ μακάριος ὑμῶν ἐπίσκοπος Σωτήρ, ὑμῶν τὴν ἐπιστολήν. Wherever we catch a glimpse of the Roman Church in these first centuries, the bishop is either out of sight or in the background. In another fragment Dionysius calls attention to the tradition that the Corinthian Church, like the Roman, had been planted by St. Peter and St. Paul. Whatever may be the truth about St. Peter's

Obscurity of the early bishops

connexion with Corinth, the fragment shows that Dionysius is ignorant of a successor of St. Peter in Rome with jurisdiction over other Churches. It is the Apostolic Church of Peter *and Paul* that is held in honour. The apocryphal Clementine literature was the instrument which prepared the way for exalting St. Peter and ignoring St. Paul.

A few years later we have evidence of a similar kind from Irenæus. In his great work against heresies, finished c. A.D. 185, he appeals, not to the Church of Rome, still less to its bishop, but to the *unbroken tradition secured in every see by a line of bishops reaching back to the Apostles.* Under God's providence it was episcopacy which preserved the Church from being destroyed by heretics and schismatics. 'We can enumerate those who were appointed bishops by the Apostles themselves in the different Churches, and their successors down to our own day; and they neither taught nor acknowledged any such stuff as is raved by these men. . . . But since it would be a long business in a work of this kind to enumerate the successions in all the Churches,' he selects as a conspicuous example that of ' the very great and ancient Church, well known to all men, founded and established by the two most glorious Apostles Peter *and Paul.*' After tracing the succession from Linus to Eleutherus, he glances at Smyrna, presided over by Polycarp, the disciple of St. John, whose Epistle to the Philippians still witnesses to his creed, and at Ephesus, founded by St. Paul and presided over by St. John down to the times of Trajan. Had there been any infallible official known to Irenæus, these appeals to various Churches,

Nature of the appeals of Irenæus

and to the security from innovation gained by unbroken succession from the Apostles, would have been senseless. In Rome this security was at a maximum. Rome was the centre of intercourse between Christians from all quarters, and any serious innovation would have been detected at once, had it occurred. And the innovations proposed by the Gnostics were no mere subtleties, but wholesale denials of fundamental doctrines about God, creation, and redemption. It was impossible that these contradictions of traditional teaching could ever have been Apostolic.

Precisely in the same manner Tertullian argues in his 'Demurrer against Heretics:' 'Run over the Apostolic Churches, in which the very Chairs of the Apostles still preside in their places, in which their own authentic writings are read, uttering the voice and representing the face of each of them. Is Achaia near you? you have Corinth. If you are not far from Macedonia, you have Philippi, you have the Thessalonians. If you can reach Asia, you have Ephesus. And if you are close to Italy, you have Rome, whence we (Carthaginians) also have an authority close at hand. Happy indeed is that Church into which Apostles poured all their doctrine with their blood, where Peter imitated the passion of the Lord; where Paul was crowned with John (the Baptist's) death; where the Apostle John was plunged into boiling oil and suffered no harm, and was then banished to an island. Let us see what it learnt, what it taught, (and how) it tallied with the Churches of Africa.' The appeal is to the traditions of all the Apostolic Churches, of which Rome is a glorious example, and for Africans the most accessible authority. 'Is it likely,' he asks, 'that Churches of such number and weight should have *strayed* into one and the same faith?'

The first person who attempted to go beyond this honourable position of the Church of Rome was Victor, the first Latin bishop. As a Roman he would feel the commanding position of a Church whose seat coincided with the seat of empire. The long peace which Christians had enjoyed under Commodus, through the influence of the φιλόθεος παλλακή Marcia, had added much to the influence of the Roman community and its leader. Once more, as in the days of Domitian, people of high position were coming over to the faith. It was natural, therefore, that a man of vigour at the head of a central and flourishing Church—confident in the correctness of his views, which were shared by the large majority of Christians, and seeing that the views of the other side were shared by a dangerous class of heretics—should go great lengths in endeavouring to gain a victory. Montanists supported the Quartadeciman practice still continued by Polycrates at Ephesus, and by other Asiatic bishops in their Churches. On the other side were the Churches of Palestine, Osrhoene, Pontus, Corinth, Gaul, and Rome. These all agreed that the 14th Nisan must give way to the Sunday, and that Easter must be celebrated only on the Lord's Day. But Victor spoilt a good and strong cause by violence. His excommunication of the Quartadeciman Churches did not induce them to yield, and was condemned by his own side, especially by his most important supporter, Irenæus. Yet in this high-handed attempt Victor proceeded by

[margin: First Roman encroachment; Victor and Polycrates]

means of Synods. Even he has no idea that the bishop of Rome as such has authority over other Churches. And other bishops have no scruple in expressing their dissent from his decision, and exhorting him with much severity to consider what will promote peace, unity, and love.

The episcopate of Victor was disturbed by other controversies which produced internal schisms. The Montanists left no one any peace; and their question became mixed up both with that about Easter and with the more serious controversies about the doctrine of the Trinity.

There were two writers of distinction in the Church of Rome at this time, Caius and Hippolytus. Of Caius nothing is really known, excepting the meagre notices of him in Eusebius and the fragments there quoted from his 'Dialogue' with the Montanist leader, Proclus. Eusebius calls him 'an orthodox person' (ἐκκλησιαστικὸς ἀνήρ), and 'very learned' (λογιώτατος). He opposed millenarian as well as Montanist doctrine. Jerome, Theodoret, and Photius simply confuse what Eusebius tells us. That Caius was a presbyter is perhaps an incorrect inference from Eusebius. Various works of unknown authorship have been attributed to Caius; among others the 'Muratorian Canon' and the 'Philosophumena' or 'Refutation of all Heresies,' the latter of which is now almost universally admitted to be by Hippolytus. Lightfoot has conjectured that, on the contrary, the 'Dialogue with Proclus' may be the work of Hippolytus, whose prænomen may have been Caius. *If* this should prove correct, then Caius, like the Presbyter John, may be banished from history as a nonentity. But the identification of Caius with Hippolytus is as yet pure conjecture.

Hippolytus is the leading theologian of the Roman Church during the second and third centuries. This is not a great distinction; for the Roman Church during this period was very unproductive of either thinkers or writers. In the hundred and thirty-six distinguished Churchmen singled out by Jerome during the first four centuries, only four are bishops of Rome. Just one in each century: Clement, Victor, Cornelius, and Damasus; and they wrote very little. The origin of Hippolytus is unknown; but his native tongue was Greek, though he seems to have lived mostly at Rome, of which Church he was a presbyter and afterwards bishop. Eusebius calls him a bishop, but rather pointedly declines to mention his see. He is often called bishop of Portus (Ostia); but Döllinger has given very strong reasons for believing that he was a schismatical bishop of Rome, set up in opposition to Callistus, whom he had discredited with many Christians by unreasonable charges of heresy and misconduct. In short, Hippolytus, rather than Novatian, must be regarded as the first antipope. The only serious objection to this view is the silence of history as to this remarkable schism in the Church of Rome. Eusebius gives the titles of some of his writings. Jerome gives another short list, not quite the same. A statue of him seated in a chair was dug up on the Via Tiburtina in 1551. On the back of the chair is another list, entirely independent of Eusebius and Jerome, and evidently original. On the side of the chair is a Paschal Cycle, which gives the full moons correctly for the

Writings of Hippolytus

years A.D. 217-223; after that it goes wrong, and soon becomes useless. The inference is that it was made c. A.D. 222, the date specified in it, and inscribed on the chair about the same time; for would any one have given it this conspicuous place after it had been proved to be quite wrong in its calculations? The statue with its list of Hippolytus's works is therefore a contemporary witness. That list does not contain the 'Refutation of all Heresies.' But both Eusebius and Jerome mention a work 'against all heresies;' and the author of the 'Refutation' mentions the Περὶ τοῦ παντός as his, and this work is in the list on the statue. Therefore the authorship of the 'Refutation' can scarcely be considered as doubtful. The Liberian Catalogue of Bishops of Rome, which Mommsen dates A.D. 354, states that 'Yppolitus presbyter' was banished with Bishop Pontianus to Sardinia in the consulship of Severus and Quintianus (A.D. 235). Probably they both died in the mines there, and hence were called martyrs. The sensational story of the poet Prudentius, that Hippolytus was torn to pieces by wild horses at Portus, is universally rejected.

The meeting of Hippolytus and Origen in Rome in the time of Zephyrinus has been already noticed (p. 77).

Relation to Tertullian and Origen

It would be interesting to know whether Hippolytus and Tertullian ever met. But Tertullian may have returned to Africa before Hippolytus established himself or became well known in Rome. These three teachers are the leading theologians of the age; and we find all three of them in an attitude of hostility to the Roman see. Tertullian certainly, and Hippolytus probably, settled down as the head of a schismatical party. Origen, though condemned by both Rome and Alexandria, continued to enjoy the full confidence of the Churches in the East. Hippolytus and Tertullian had much in common—in their attitude towards the bishop of Rome, their sympathy with millenarian views, their contention against any relaxations in Church discipline, and their doctrine of the Trinity. It is possible that there is more than an accidental resemblance between the treatise of Hippolytus against Noëtus and that of Tertullian against Praxeas. Nevertheless, Hippolytus regarded Tertullian as a schismatic on account of his Montanism, and hence was drawn more towards Origen as an opponent of Noëtus, and as having been excommunicated by the Roman Church.

Zephyrinus and Callistus are the first bishops of Rome of whose personal history and character we have contemporary information. But it is so coloured by prejudice that it requires to be read with much caution. The student will gain a more correct view from Döllinger's skilful analysis of it than from the bare narrative of Hippolytus himself.

Hippolytus and Callistus

The episcopate of Urban (c. A.D. 222-230) is eventless. Alexander Severus left the Church in peace externally: internally it remained disturbed by the schism created by Hippolytus. This schism probably came to an end when both Hippolytus and Bishop Pontianus were banished by Maximin the Thracian, the first barbarian emperor, to the mines in Sardinia, A.D. 235. The fact that he ended his days in this frightful kind of imprisonment, side by side with the bishop whom he opposed, is perhaps the reason why Hippolytus has been remembered as a theologian and a

Death of Hippolytus

martyr, rather than as the leader of a schism and the first antipope.

Anteros, Pontian's successor, was quickly followed by Fabian, who found a martyr's death in the Decian per-
Martyrdom of Fabian secution, A.D. 250. He is said to have divided the regions of the city among the deacons, and to have made considerable constructions in the Catacombs. He was one of the many bishops to whom Origen wrote in defence of his orthodoxy. The persecution prevented the election of a successor, and the see remained vacant for more than a year.

During this vacancy we have the notable correspondence between the Churches of Rome and Africa in
Roman see vacant which Novatian and Cyprian take the lead. It is conducted in Latin; and with Novatian the Latin literature of the Roman Church fairly begins. The Roman letter is addressed 'to *Pope* Cyprian.'[1]

The Roman Church was scarcely free from one schism
Novatian schism when it was troubled by another. About March A.D. 251 Cornelius was almost unanimously elected, and he reluctantly accepted the dangerous post. Cyprian praises his courage, and states that Decius would sooner hear of a rival emperor than of a new bishop of Rome. But Decius was away on the Gothic campaign which cost him his life. His death soon caused the persecution to cease; and forthwith arose the question how to deal with the many weak Christians who in one way or other had yielded under its pressure. Among them were not a few clergy, against whom Decius had directed special efforts. The mitigation of discipline

[1] Cypriano *Papæ* presbyteri et diaconi Romæ consistentes salutem.

introduced by Callistus with regard to other gross sins influenced the decision of this question about the *lapsed*. The Roman clergy both before and after the election of Cornelius were against the extreme measure of absolute excommunication. In this they were opposed by the leading presbyter Novatian. At Carthage a schismatic of similar name (Novatus) and similar views had appeared; and when he crossed over to Rome, Novatian was consecrated as a rival bishop to Cornelius by three Italian bishops. His sect called themselves *Cathari* or Purists. Eusebius (who like most Greeks calls Novatian, Novatus — Νοουάτος or Ναυάτος) quotes parts of a letter from Cornelius to Fabius of Antioch, in which he states that, numerous as are the clergy and laity in Rome, they have been unable to persuade Novatian to give way. Cornelius gives most interesting statistics. The Catholic Church of Rome, he says, possesses one (and of course only one) bishop, forty-six presbyters, seven deacons, seven sub-deacons, forty-two acolythes, fifty-two exorcists, readers, and door-keepers, and more than 1,500 widows and orphans who are supported by the Church. This statement is thought to imply a total of 30,000 Christians in Rome. Fabius of Antioch was rather inclined to Novatian, but died before the Synod at Antioch decided against the rigorist view. The schism at Carthage and at Rome brought Cyprian and Cornelius closer together. Cyprian was disposed to be a rigorist himself; but, as he believed that there was no salvation outside the Church, to refuse communion to fallen Christians was to anticipate the final judgment of God. Therefore, without exactly condemning the views of Novatian, he agreed with Corne-

THE CHURCHES IN ITALY 103

lius and the majority of bishops in condemning his schismatical action.

Gallus, the successor of Decius, revived the persecution, and Cornelius with most of the Christians in Rome retired into Etruria. Cornelius died there, at Centumcellæ. Lucius, his successor, was banished immediately, A.D. 253, but soon returned, and many Christians returned with him. The Novatianists appear to have been undisturbed. And Cyprian regards it as a mark of the true Chruch and true bishop that Cornelius and Lucius with their flock were singled out for persecution, and not the heretics, *quibus diabolus ut suis parceret*. Under Stephen Novatianism steadily declined.

<small>Decline of Novatianism</small>

The episcopate of Stephen is marked by high-handed action on the part of the Roman bishop which recalls the conduct of Victor towards Polycrates (see p. 96). Two Spanish bishops, Basilides and Martial, had fallen away in the Decian persecution and committed other offences. Basilides abdicated, and successors were appointed in both their sees. They went to Rome and induced Stephen to attempt to restore them; and some bishops admitted them to communion. Their own clergy appealed to Cyprian against Stephen. A Synod at Carthage A.D. 254 replied that Stephen had been deceived by the apostates, and that Sabinus and Felix, who had been consecrated in their place, were the rightful holders of the sees. Again, Faustinus of Lyons and other bishops informed Stephen that Marcianus of Arles had become a Novatianist. Stephen took no notice. Whereupon Faustinus wrote to Cyprian, and the latter sent Stephen a rather sharp letter urging him to advise the Gallican bishops

<small>Second Roman encroachment; Stephen and Cyprian</small>

to remove Marcian and substitute a successor. Then came the question of the admission of converted heretics; but we no longer know how it arose. Ought such persons to be rebaptized, as Synods at Carthage under Agrippinus (c. A.D. 220) and at Iconium and Synnada, (c. A.D. 230), had determined, or merely receive imposition of hands, as was the custom at Rome? Some African bishops suspected that rebaptizing was wrong, because the Novatianists baptized presbyters from the Church. Cyprian assures them that in this Novatian is only aping the Catholic practice, and three Synods at Carthage (c. A.D. 255, 256) decided that baptism should continue to be the practice of their Church. No attempt was made to dictate to others; but Stephen, who had already broken off communion with some Asiatic Churches about this question, now excommunicated the Africans and denounced Cyprian as 'a false Christ, a false Apostle, and a deceitful worker.'[1] Cyprian wrote to the Asiatic Churches; and Firmilian of Cæsarea in Cappadocia, the friend of Origen, wrote in the strongest terms against both the conduct and the character of Stephen. The death of Stephen, A.D. 257, mitigated the controversy, and Dionysius of Alexandria mediated with his successor Xystus. The Roman practice was eventually upheld by the eighth canon of the Council of Arles (A.D. 314), and by implication by the eighth Canon of Nicæa. Augustine argues strongly against rebaptism in his treatise against the Donatists. But the

---

[1] Firmilian, *Ep. ad Cypr.* (26). The Epistle contains the earliest reference to 2 Peter that is at all probable. It speaks of Peter and Paul execrating heretics (6), and in 1 Peter there is no execration of false teachers.

important thing to notice is that, not only do both Cyprian and Firmilian condemn Stephen's action in very plain language, but no one, not even Stephen himself, considers the decision of the Roman bishop or the Roman Church final. The appeal is to analogous cases in Scripture, to ancient tradition, and to reason. And Stephen broke off communion with the Asiatic and African Churches, not because they refused obedience to Rome, but because they rebaptized heretics, an error which he regarded as fundamental.

No Emperor, says Dionysius of Alexandria, had been more friendly to the Christians than Valerian was at first. 'All his house was full of worshippers, and was a Church of God.' It was Macrianus who stirred him up to become a persecutor. In this persecution both Xystus and Cyprian perished, A.D. 258.

Of Dionysius, the successor of Xystus, enough has been said in connexion with his namesake of Alexandria (see p. 85). He was followed, A.D. 269, by Felix, in whose episcopate the appeal to Aurelian about Paul of Samosata, and the Emperor's decision to refer the case to the bishops of Italy and Rome, took place. Three spurious decretals have been assigned to him. Eutychianus (A.D. 275) and Caius (A.D. 283) are little more than names. Marcellinus (A.D. 296–304) lived to see the beginning of the Diocletian persecution. With him is connected the fable of the Synod of Sinuessa. He is said to have sacrificed during the persecution. A Council of 300 bishops (!) met to consider the case and laid down the principle that he *could only be judged by himself*; whereupon he abdicated. This is the object of the clumsy fable; to

Alleged apostacy of Marcellinus

bolster the claim of Popes to be above the law. It was probably forged c. A.D. 500. But the story of his sacrificing may be true. This charge was made by Donatists in Augustine's day. He scouts it; but he says nothing stronger than that it is unsupported by documentary evidence; and that people about whom we know nothing ought to be considered innocent.[1] The chronology here becomes obscure again, partly owing to the similarity of name between Marcellinus and his successor Marcellus; but there was a vacancy of several years between the two.

The episcopate of Marcellus (c. A.D. 307–309) is marked by a renewal of the question about those who Fresh disturbances had lapsed under persecution. Marcellus insisted on the usual discipline of a period of serious penance. Many contended for speedy readmission. The controversy led to blows and even bloodshed; and this perhaps explains why Marcellus is sometimes spoken of as a confessor and a martyr. His successor Eusebius was banished to Sicily by Maxentius, and died there after a pontificate of a few months. Miltiades or Melchiades followed after another interval of nearly a year. The disturbed state of the Roman Church and of the Roman Empire fully accounts for the vacancy. How the question of the lapsed was solved we do not know; but the triumph of Constantine (A.D. 312), and the Edict of Milan, granting full toleration to Christianity (A.D. 313), would be occasions for granting something like a general amnesty, even if this had not already taken place when Galerius and his colleagues

[1] Döllinger leaves the question open; *Fables respecting the Popes*, pp. 79–85, Eng. ed. Lightfoot is inclined to disbelieve the charge

THE CHURCHES IN ITALY

published the first edict of toleration at Nicomedia some nine months after the election of Miltiades. The latter part of the episcopate of Miltiades was troubled by the rise of the Donatist controversy, the history of which lies outside our period. He died early in 314, and with him this sketch of the Roman Church ends.

Of the other Churches in Italy we have very little information at this early period. The *Libellus Synodicus* gives four Councils held at Rome in the second century.

Fictitious Councils

1. Under Telesphorus against Theodotus the Tanner.
2. Under Anicetus about the Paschal question.
3. Under Victor against Theodotus, Ebion, and Artemon.
4. Under Victor against Sabellius and Noëtus.

All these are probably fictitious. There is no sufficient evidence of any of them. Theodotus did not come to Rome till fifty years after Telesphorus, and Sabellius was still uncondemned under Victor's successor, Zephyrinus. He was excommunicated in the time of Callistus. The conference between Anicetus and Polycarp has been magnified into a Council.

Jerome and Rufinus state that an assembly at Rome condemned Origen. They probably mean in the time of Pontianus. But we are not sure that the statement is correct; and, if it is, *senatus* need not mean more than an assembly of the Roman clergy. It gives us no information about the bishops of Italy.

A *senatus* against Origen

We are on firmer ground when we come to the Council held by Cornelius c. A.D. 251 about the lapsed and about Novatian. At this Eusebius tells us that sixty bishops were present, with a still larger number of presbyters and deacons. These sixty bishops would be mostly from Italian sees; but we have no list of them. Quite small towns in some cases had a bishop.

A council about the lapsed

Hefele gives a Roman Council held under Dionysius A.D. 260 to consider the language used by his namesake of Alexandria in opposing Paul of Samosata (see p. 85). This Synod seems to be a mere conjecture; an inference, probably erroneous, from the facts.

CHAPTER VII.

THE CHURCHES IN NORTH AFRICA.

LIKE the Church in Gaul, the Church in *Africa* bursts upon us suddenly towards the end of the second century. The planting and growth in each case is hidden from us; but when the veil is raised we find a large and vigorous Christian community already in existence. The history of the Gallican Church begins with the letter of the Christians in Vienne and Lyons to those in Asia and Phrygia respecting the martyrdoms in the persecution of A.D. 177: that of the African Church begins just twenty years later with the 'Apologeticus' of Tertullian. But in the latter case there is both more to know and far better means of knowing it than in the former. In the priceless information which Irenæus gives us in his writings there is singularly little about the Church of which he was overseer for more than

Origin of the African Church unknown

THE CHURCHES IN NORTH AFRICA 109

twenty years. In the writings of Tertullian, the Church of Africa—hitherto unknown in history—is suddenly placed before us with a fulness and vividness scarcely equalled by any Church at this period, and exceeded by none.

Africa, like Asia, is a name which increased in meaning as geographical knowledge increased: each from Province of indicating a small territory at last extended to Africa a whole continent. In our period Africa means the Roman province of Africa, which, since the time of Caligula, had included Numidia and extended from the river Ampsaga to the Great Syrtis. Of this province Carthage was the centre; and, just as the history of the Churches in Italy is practically the history of the Church of Rome, so that of the Churches in Africa is concentrated in the Church of Carthage.

Africa was a most prosperous province. It was seldom devastated by internal war. The revolt of the Its Gordians (A.D. 238) was very quickly extinprosperity guished, and then commerce and agriculture went on as before. This prosperous tranquillity favoured the spread of Christianity during the second century. When and whence the Gospel first reached Africa is quite unknown; but by A.D. 200 it is widespread, vigorous, and enterprising. Carthage was probably an early centre from which Christianity spread over Numidia and Mauritania.

Carthage reminds us of Corinth, which was destroyed (B.C. 146) and refounded (B.C. 46) along with it. In Character- both we have a very mixed population: a popuistics of Carthage lation without an aristocracy, mainly devoted to commerce, knowing few social distinctions but those of wealth, and under all the demoralising influences of a seaport. In both we find a restless mental activity, which intensified controversy and promoted schism, tendencies which were still further aggravated at Carthage by hot African blood and a fiery climate. This, however, had its bright side also. Christianity, ardently embraced, was ardently cherished and defended; the fervid African spirit found expression in energetic benevolence, in stern self-discipline, and in heroic courage. If sectarianism was nowhere more aggressive, persecution was nowhere more unflinchingly endured.

The African Church forms a marked contrast to its neighbour in Alexandria. The latter was Eastern, the former Western, in character. The African despised a transcendentalism which seemed unpractical and unreal. The heresies which attracted him—Montanism, Novatianism, and Donatism—were more moral than speculative; and when he became speculative it was about himself rather than about the universe or its Creator. Psychology had a practical bearing on conduct; metaphysics had not. There was reason in discussing the nature of the soul, its freedom, and its relation to divine grace. Mysteries of the Godhead or the nature of Christ were to be accepted without reasoning. This contrast reaches a climax when Tertullian—one of the most argumentative of men—suddenly surrenders reason in his famous *credo quia absurdum*.

Contrast with Alexandria

As the history of the Egyptian Church is concentrated in Clement of Alexandria and Origen, and that of the Gallican in Irenæus, so the Church of Africa has its life summed up in the work of

Its great men

three great men, Tertullian, Cyprian, and Augustine. After Origen, no writers have had more effect upon the development of Christianity than these three. Only the first two come within our period.

Quintus Septimius Florens Tertullianus was born, probably at Carthage, c. A.D. 150. His father was a centurion in the service of the proconsul. His wide acquaintance with very various branches of literature proves that he had received an excellent education, and he seems to have studied law and to have practised at the bar. Eusebius speaks of his intimate knowledge of Roman jurisprudence. He is fond of legal terms, and his style of arguing is that of the impassioned advocate. If his profession taught him how to recognise evidence, it also taught him how to make the very most of it. Of the details of his life we know nothing. For the first half of his life he was a heathen, and lived in heathen wickedness. But when (c. A.D. 185) he became a Christian, he did so with the passionate enthusiasm and intense conviction that characterizes all he says and does It was doubtless as the result of personal experience that he maintained that 'Christians are made, not born,' and that 'the human soul in its very nature is Christian.' He became a presbyter, but, like Clement and Origen, he never advanced beyond that rank; and he was married. Both facts have been questioned, in order to get rid of a married presbyter among the strictest of rigorists; but without sufficient reason. His own works are conclusive as to his marriage, but leave his position in the Church less certain. Jerome tells us that he was a presbyter; and this is probable in itself, and is not contradicted by

Tertullian

the rhetorical question, 'Are not even we laymen priests?'[1] Here he argumentatively ranges himself with the laity. In the strange passage in which he contends that the soul has form and colour ('De Anim.' ix.) he apparently separates himself from the laity. After a sermon from him the congregation departed, and an ecstatic woman told him that during the sacred rites she had been shown a soul in a bodily shape. Some portion of his life was spent in Rome; but we do not know when or for how long he was there. The length of his stay would seem to have been considerable: long enough to make him acquainted with a Latin Version of the Scriptures which sometimes differs widely from that used at Carthage by Cyprian. While Cyprian's text is African, that of Tertullian seems to be sometimes African, and sometimes European. Moreover, his knowledge of the affairs of the Roman Church is probably due to his long stay among them. Jerome says that it was the envy and contumely of the Roman clergy which drove Tertullian to become a Montanist 'after remaining a presbyter of the Church until he reached middle age.' This implies that he was a presbyter of the Church for some years and a member of the Church still longer. Hence Pusey's date for his conversion (A.D. 196) seems to be too late; for his lapse into Montanism cannot be placed later than A.D. 203. The arrogance of the Roman clergy may have been the proximate cause of his separation from the Church; but he may be almost said to be a born Montanist. The fanatical enthusiasm, the stern Church discipline, and the austere asceticism

---

[1] Nonne et laici sacerdotes sumus? *De Exhort. Cast.* vii. Comp. Cum extollimur et inflamur adversus clerum; *De Monog.* xii.

which characterized Montanism were entirely in harmony with his fiery and gloomy temperament. And he made Montanism not merely respectable, but a power with which both churchmen and heretics had to reckon. While the passion for a stricter discipline than he found in the Church seduced him into schism, yet he ever remained true to the Church's faith. Some of his most telling works against Gnosticism and other heretics were written after he became a schismatic; and his scorching eloquence is far more effective against the common foe than against the communion which he had left. He contends vehemently that, 'provided the rule of faith remain intact, all other matters of discipline and conversation admit of development and change, with the assistance of God's grace. For what a monstrous position that, while the devil is ever working and adding daily to the devices of iniquity, the work of God has failed, or ceased to advance.' 'Our Lord Christ has called Himself Truth, not tradition.' Increase in strictness of life was indicated by Christ when He said, 'I have many things to say unto you, but ye cannot bear them now.' There is no heresy in mere change of discipline. The heretic changes doctrine, and thence goes on to change of discipline.—All which is excellent; but the question remains whether individuals have the right to construct a new discipline not only for themselves but for the Church, and to separate from the Church if the discipline is not adopted.

Jerome calls Tertullian a man *acris et vehementis ingenii*; and the epithets are well deserved. Tertullian bewails his own habitual heat of temper: *Miserrimus ego semper æger caloribus impa-*

His violent temper

C. H. I

tientiæ, quam non obtineo patientiæ sanitatem et suspirem et invocem et perorem necesse est. And this fault had much to do with his fall. That the Roman clergy should be relaxing Church discipline (see p. 102) at the very time when he and others wished to tighten it, seemed to him intolerable, and he washed his hands of all who did tolerate it. Nor did he content himself with this extreme method of protest. He attacked those whom he deserted with all the adroitness of an advocate and all the bitterness of a pervert. Catholics, no less than heathen, Jews, and heretics, were now pursued with every kind of argument, fair and unfair, with sarcasms, with insinuations, and abuse. And there is a marked difference of tone in his writings before and after his separation. The self-confident impatience which was natural to him was intensified by secession, and the vehement opposer of error sinks down into the arrogant reviler of the Church. He is a conspicuous instance of those who think that unchastened language is the best means of inculcating a chastened life.

His style matches his thought. It abounds in outrageous and outlandish expressions, but is vigorous, emphatic, and eloquent. His terseness and abruptness make him sometimes obscure, and his vocabulary is amazing in its indiscriminateness. No term is too technical or archaic, no expression too vulgar or provincial, if only it will indicate his meaning. And where a Latin word is not ready to his hand, he tries Greek or coins a fresh one. His style has all the mingled material and all the rapidity and directness of an avalanche. Timber, stone, and earth, leaves, flowers, and rubbish, are all swept together and hurled along,

[margin: The creator of ecclesiastical Latin]

to open out some choked path or to overwhelm an adversary. In all this, whether he himself was aware of it or not, he was making a new language, the language of ecclesiastical Latin. Minucius Felix probably preceded him; but the literature of Latin Christianity really begins with Tertullian. He had ideas to express which had never been expressed in Latin before, and his one aim is to express them forcibly. If this can be done in good Latin, well; if not, by whatever violence to taste, syntax, and vocabulary, forcibly expressed they must be.

Many of his writings are lost, especially his earlier ones and those written in Greek; but those which remain are numerous, though for the most part short. They are 'Tracts for the Times,' and cover a great multitude of subjects, apologetical, polemical, doctrinal, moral, and social. They give a vivid picture of Christian and heathen life at the close of the second century, especially in North Africa, and are of the utmost value to the historian. It is scarcely a paradox to say that they are all the more valuable owing to his lapse into schism. His secession led him to attack what he considered to be defective in the Church; and he thus gives information respecting discipline and practice which would otherwise have been omitted. But perhaps no writings require to be read with greater caution. One must always remember that one is listening to the special pleading of an impassioned advocate, not to the sworn testimony of a witness or the summing up of a judge. If one were to single out three of the most important of his works, one would name the 'Apologeticus,' written when he was in the

His chief writings

Church, the 'Adversus Marcionem,' written (A.D. 207) after he had left it, and the ' De Præscriptione Hæreticorum,' which is doubtful. They illustrate his method of dealing with paganism, with Gnosticism, and with heresy in general, and with his other writings form one of the main links in the chain which connects the age of Augustine with the age of St. John.

Neither the manner nor the date of his death is known; it may be placed anywhere between A.D. 220 and 240. Jerome says he lived to be very old. The statement that he returned to the Church is rendered improbable by the fact that two centuries later Augustine writes gently of the Tertullianists as a sect that was just expiring. Probably Tertullian left the Montanists without formally returning to the Church. It may be doubted whether he ever accepted the whole teaching of Montanus; and he was perhaps rather claimed by the sect than definitely received into it. A man of his ability was well worth claiming. On the other hand, there was much in so illiterate a sect as the Montanists which must have been very distasteful to a person of his culture and learning. As he was never excommunicated (a fact which says much for the forbearance of those whom he so mercilessly assailed), he may have considered that no formal restoration was necessary. There is at least some ground for hoping that his last years were free from active hostility against the Church of which he might have been the strongest defender.

A comparison of Tertullian with Origen is most interesting and instructive, and it may be carried out into great detail. Only a few broad features can be noticed here. Both were highly original, and in ability and influence were incomparably the leading Christians of their time; yet were presbyters and no more in the Churches of which they were the most distinguished members. Both led lives of the strictest self-denial and of great literary activity, producing writings which have been an abundant source of enlightenment, edification, and perplexity to the Church. Both were staunch defenders of the faith against heathen, Jews, and heretics, and alike by precept and example taught others to be willing to suffer rather than compromise it. Yet both spent the latter portion of their devoted lives cut off from the greater part of Christendom, and in an attitude of opposition to those in authority over them. These points of marked resemblance are on the surface; but there are points of still more marked difference which lie deeper. That the one spent half his life in pagan wickedness, while the other from his birth had the blessing of a beautiful Christian home, is the explanation of much that follows. The gloomy fervour of the stern African was doubtless in his blood; but it was intensified by the complete break with the past which his conversion imposed upon him; whereas the 'sweetness and light' of the lovable Alexandrian was an unbroken development of Christian graces. Akin to this difference is the contrast between the dogmatic positiveness of the one and the speculative suggestiveness of the other. Both in form and in spirit, the writings of the two, even on similar subjects, are widely different. In the one writer truth is in danger of being strangled in the letter, in the other of being lost in lofty aspiration.

Tertullian the antithesis of Origen

To the moral despair of the world Tertullian offers sternness, to its intellectual despair a scoff. Origen has deep sympathy for both—the sympathy of a self-sacrificing life and of an undaunted search after truth. To a certain extent Origen's position is a reaction from that of Tertullian. It is in combating literal anthropomorphic conceptions of God, materialistic views about the soul, and gross forms of Millenarianism—all of which were favoured by Tertullian—that Origen is apt to run into extremes. Tertullian had sympathy with Montanism and intense hostility to Gnosticism; the sympathies of Origen are exactly the other way. Tertullian, who had studied philosophy as a heathen, had an utter contempt for it; Origen, who had studied it (and far more thoroughly) as a Christian, highly esteemed it. The one regarded it as rubbish, which must make way for the Gospel; the other, as a partial and preparatory revelation, which might still serve as a handmaid to the truth. Further contrasts in their teaching about the Godhead, the nature of Christ, sin, and the future state might be added; but these must suffice. In conclusion, we must remember the essential difference which underlies the apparent similarity of their relations to their respective Churches. Tertullian's separation was his own doing; that of Origen was the work of his adversaries. Tertullian, though never condemned at Carthage, deliberately left and attacked the Church in which he had ministered. Origen, excommunicated at Alexandria and Rome, lived on in closest communion with the Churches in the East, and died—virtually a martyr's death—in the midst of them.

Of bishops of Carthage during the time of Tertullian

THE CHURCHES IN NORTH AFRICA 119

we know singularly little. Under Agrippinus was held
First Council of Carthage the first Council of Carthage, c. A.D. 220. It decreed the rebaptizing of heretics. But
Morcelli places the Council as early as A.D. 197, and the death of Agrippinus A.D. 200. He gives Optatus and Cyrus as bishops of Carthage between Agrippinus and Cyprian. There were seventy bishops of Africa and Numidia at the Council, showing the flourishing state of the Church in Africa at this time. Probably Spain, Gaul, Italy, and Egypt together could hardly have produced so large a gathering. Of course the dioceses were small. Seventy sees do not imply much territory.

If Tertullian is the great controversialist, Cyprian is the great prelate of his age. It is as an overseer
Cyprian's relation to Tertullian of the Church, as a ruler, an organiser, and an administrator, that Cyprian shows his consummate ability. Thascius Cyprianus was born c. A.D. 200, about the time when Tertullian separated from the Church. Like him he was brought up a heathen, had a liberal education, studied law and rhetoric, and practised oratory. His, therefore, was another highly cultivated mind gained for the Church. He is said to have been gifted with an excellent memory, which is confirmed by the abundant quotations in his writings. In those days of papyrus-rolls without numbered divisions it was no easy matter to look out and copy quotations. He was wealthy; but his heathen life, unlike Tertullian's, seems to have been free from vice. He was converted about A.D. 245 by an old presbyter, whose name—Cæcilianus—he took at his baptism. He was already writing in the interests of

the Gospel his 'De Idolorum Vanitate,' 'Testimonia adv. Judæos,' and 'Ad Donatum.' In the two former he borrows freely from Minucius Felix and Tertullian. Jerome tells us that Cyprian used daily to ask for Tertullian's works with the words, '*Da magistrum*—Hand me the master;' and his indebtedness to Tertullian elsewhere, especially in the 'De Patientia,' is marked. In making use of 'the master' he tones down his strained expressions and smooths his rugged language; but he never mentions him. Tertullian's was a name too full of painful associations; and by implication Cyprian's theory of the Church condemns Tertullian. One detail in which they dissented from one another is characteristic of each of them. The severe Tertullian had contended that the philosopher's *pallium* was the most suitable dress for a Christian. The refined Cyprian thought its simplicity affected. That the two knew one another personally is possible, but uncertain.

About two years after the baptism of Cyprian, the Bishop of Carthage died. The laity and a majority of the clergy urged Cyprian to accept the office. He declined, and meditated flight. This was prevented, and the populace would accept no refusal. In spite of his being still a neophyte (1 Tim. iii. 6), he was elected, like Ambrose and Augustine, by popular acclamation. The choice was a prudent one, and was amply justified by results. Cyprian had position, wealth, learning, and literary ability. What was of still greater moment, he was known as a person of high character, generosity, tact, and decision, and as an excellent man of business. Five presbyters opposed the elec-

[margin: Cyprian elected bishop]

tion, but they were overruled; and between July 248 and April 249 Cyprian was consecrated. The neighbouring bishops approved the election. Cyprian regarded it as 'God's decree.' That he is now addressed even by the Roman clergy as 'pope' (*papa*) has been already noticed. The title was used of bishops of Alexandria and of Carthage before it was applied to the bishops of Rome.

The first eighteen months of Cyprian's episcopate were the last eighteen months of the 'thirty years' peace.' For many years the Churches had enjoyed comparative freedom from persecution and the results were by no means all good. Christianity had spread; but it counted many weak and unworthy characters among its adherents. Perhaps nowhere was this more the case than in prosperous Africa. Serious scandals existed even among the clergy. Bishops were farmers, traders, and money-lenders, and by no means always honest. Some were too ignorant to teach catechumens. Presbyters made money by helping in the manufacture of idols. The way in which Tertullian and Cyprian—like Clement of Alexandria—inveigh against luxury and extravagance in dress and food proves that well-to-do Christians were very numerous, and that easy circumstances produced laxity of life. A sharp remedy was needed; and Cyprian believed that he was divinely warned of the trial that was coming. At the end of A.D. 249 the Decian persecution broke out. In accordance with Christ's direction (Matt. x. 23), Cyprian retired before it. His life was necessary for the direction of the Church, and his presence in Carthage would have increased the suffer-

Declan persecution

Cyprian's flight

ings inflicted on the community. The number of apostates was immense. Many sacrificed at once (*thurificati, sacrificati*). Many more bought certificates of having sacrificed, although they had not really done so (*libellatici*), or got their names placed upon the lists of those who had satisfied the authorities (*acta facientes*). On the other hand, there were numbers of noble confessors and martyrs, who endured confiscation, banishment, imprisonment, torture, and death rather than by word or act deny Christ. Cyprian wrote, urging prudence and moderation. Caution must be used in visiting confessors in prison; the heathen must not be provoked. There were Montanist fanatics ready to challenge the persecutors, in order to secure martyrdom at any cost. This form of fanaticism was not confined to the Montanists; and in some cases the motive may have been a good one. Men may have hoped to prove to the persecutors that their policy was a hopeless one. What use was there in hunting down a people who actually courted death? The Montanists joined with those who had opposed Cyprian's election, and denounced him as a runaway both in Carthage and at Rome. The Roman clergy wrote to Cyprian, informing him of the martyrdom of their own bishop, Fabian; and also sent another letter to the Carthaginian clergy saying sarcastically that Cyprian, as a *persona insignis*, no doubt did rightly in retiring; but it is the hireling that seeth the wolf coming and fleeth, and they hope that their Carthaginian brethren will not be found hirelings. Cyprian replied to both, sending back the insulting letter with a courteous request that they would examine it and see whether it is what they wrote; he thinks it may have been tampered with. He also sent a full statement respecting his conduct.

His flight, like his election, was amply justified by the result. The persecution involved the Church in difficulties which required a master mind to deal with them. These were of two opposite kinds, both affecting discipline. There were the numerous confessors who had suffered banishment or torture or imprisonment, and who were in some cases quite thrown off their balance by their victory. They were held in such honour that their heads were turned. They were looked upon as singularly holy, as perfect saints; and there was serious danger that transitory suffering would be regarded as of more value than a holy life, and that confessorship would afford a reason, or at least an excuse, for subsequent self-indulgence. On the other hand, there were numerous apostates clamouring to be readmitted to communion, and entreating the confessors to intercede for them. These frequently granted to the lapsed 'certificates of peace' (*libelli pacis*). These certificates were regarded by the recipients as equivalent to absolution, or as constituting a claim to it; and Cyprian hints that they were sometimes bought. They were sometimes vaguely comprehensive. 'Let this man with his friends (*cum suis*) be admitted to communion.' Cyprian tells the confessors that they must give the name of every one whom they recommend for restoration, and must take heed that they recommend only those who by penitence have proved themselves worthy. Cyprian at first was disposed to be very stern with the lapsed, like Tertullian before him at Carthage, and Novatian

His justification

Difficulties about the lapsed

his contemporary at Rome; refusing readmission even on the eve of death. It was difficult to make such severity agree with his own theory that outside the Church there is no salvation; for no one maintained that a penitent apostate could not be saved. Moreover, the large number of the lapsed and the more moderate view of other Churches, especially of Rome, compelled him to modify his position. And when once any were readmitted on their death-bed, further relaxation became necessary. Some who had been readmitted in extreme sickness recovered; and then it was impossible to keep others excommunicated who were not more guilty, but had not chanced to fall ill. A Council in 251 decided that penitent *libellatici* might be restored, but that *sacrificati* must submit to a long penance, distinctions being drawn between those who had sacrificed voluntarily and those who had done so under torture, and also between those who had made their families share their apostasy and those who had apostatised in order to save their families. Clergy who had lapsed, even when restored, must not perform any clerical function. Five deposed bishops helped to generate a schism.

The opposition to Cyprian had by no means died out. His flight and the controversy about the lapsed accentuated it. The ringleaders were the presbyter Novatus and the deacon Felicissimus, with the five dissentient presbyters. Novatus went to Rome and supported the party of Novatian in their schismatical opposition to the duly elected Bishop Cornelius and to the relaxation of severity towards the lapsed. Felicissimus got five deposed bishops to ordain

Cyprian's troubles

THE CHURCHES IN NORTH AFRICA 125

Fortunatus, one of the presbyters, as a rival bishop of Carthage. But very few people recognised Fortunatus, and the schism came to an end.

Another Council at Carthage in May 252 made still further relaxations respecting the lapsed. Gallus having succeeded Decius, persecution was again imminent; and how could Christians prepare for the storm if they were deprived of the sacraments? Therefore all who were repentant were at once restored.

Council of A.D. 252

That same year the plague, which had already been desolating Ethiopia and Egypt, reached Carthage. It raged in different parts of the world for twenty years, very fiercely at Alexandria and Carthage. It brought out the self-devotion of the Christians in their care for the sick and the dead in contrast to the selfish fears of the heathen. Cyprian describes the symptoms, tells Christians they must expect no exemption from the visitation, and that those who die in it are set free from this world. To the wicked it is a plague, to God's servants it is salvation. He rebukes the inconsistency of putting on black for the dead. Should black clothes be put on here when they have already assumed white robes there? Will not the heathen fairly blame us for mourning as extinct and lost those who we declare are alive with God?

Plague at Carthage

In A.D. 254 Stephen became bishop of Rome. His arrogant conduct towards the African Church in the controversy about rebaptizing heretics has been already related (p. 104). He declared that he would hold no communion with Churches which practised rebaptism. Whereupon Firmilian of Cæsarea told

Question of rebaptizing heretics

him that he had excommunicated himself. The arguments used on both sides are most interesting, but cannot here be recounted. The appeal was to Scripture, to Apostolical tradition, and to reason. Since Nicæa the whole Church has decided that on the question of rebaptism Stephen was right and Cyprian wrong. God's family is larger than the Church's communion. Those who have been baptized by heretical ministers are His children and members of Christ. But, on the larger question of charity and unity in spite of serious diversity, Cyprian was right and Stephen wrong. Churches may differ widely on important points without severing communion. That the African Councils on the question did not represent the unanimous opinion of the African Church is proved by the anonymous treatise 'On Rebaptism,' and by the ease with which their decisions were afterwards cancelled. As at the Vatican Council, there seems to have been a minority who voted with Cyprian, not because they were convinced, but because they did not wish to oppose.

In 256 Valerian was stirred up by Macrianus to renew the persecution. Stephen died the same year, and was succeeded by a *bonus et pacificus sacerdos*, as Pontius, Cyprian's deacon and biographer, rather pointedly calls Xystus. Cyprian was banished from Carthage, as Dionysius from Alexandria, but was treated with consideration at Curubis, where he heard of the martyrdom of Xystus in August 258. He returned to Carthage to be examined by the proconsul under the second and more severe edict of Valerian. The proceedings lasted a month. September 14, the proconsul, after vain endeavours to persuade

Martyrdom of Cyprian

him to recant, sentenced him to be beheaded. Cyprian's sole reply was *Deo gratias*. Crowds followed him to his execution. In 250 the mob had shouted *Cyprianus ad leonem!* Now they pitied and honoured him. His conduct during the plague had won them over. He prayed, removed his upper garment, and ordered twenty gold pieces to be given to the executioner. He bound his own eyes, and his clergy bound his hands. His body was buried on the spot, but was afterwards removed by night and entombed with much pomp. He seems to have been the first bishop of Carthage who suffered martyrdom.

Even in his death Cyprian is still the great prelate. The heathen no less than the faithful seem to have recognised in him a prince among men, and to have shown him marked respect. It is easy with Gibbon to sneer at all this. But a man who can fill a great office with dignity and success, winning the admiration of even outsiders and foes, is one whom the world and the Church can alike revere. Let us make the most of the honours and comforts with which Cyprian to the last was surrounded; they do but enhance the merit of his readiness to part with them. It is against all the evidence that we have, to represent the respect with which he was treated by the proconsul as a specimen 'of the spirit and form of the Roman persecutions;' and equally illogical to argue that the high honours paid to such martyrs 'betray the inconsiderable number of those who died for the profession of Christianity.' Civilisation would have been the poorer if the Church had never possessed rulers like Cyprian and Hildebrand; and those who honoured them in their lifetime have but anticipated the verdict of posterity.

Of the successors of Cyprian in the see of Carthage very little is known. Carpophorus and Lucian are mere names. Mensurius was bishop during the Diocletian persecution, and is remarkable for two things. (1) When he was ordered to deliver up his copies of the Scriptures, he hid them and passed off some heretical books in their place. (2) He and his archdeacon Cæcilian endeavoured to put a stop to the extravagant honour that was paid to confessors. Numbers of disreputable persons got themselves imprisoned as Christians, and were supported and petted in their confinement by fanatical admirers. The craze for martyrdom and martyrs had been steadily on the increase among the fervid Africans. To become a martyr, like becoming a Crusader in a later age, was believed to compensate for a life of sin and to be a substitute for repentance; and martyrs and their relics received boundless reverence. Mensurius and Cæcilian were vehemently opposed in their endeavours to check this evil; and when Cæcilian became bishop of Carthage A.D. 311 the opposition elected a rival bishop, Majorinus, and the Donatist schism was the result.

<small>Beginning of the Donatist schism</small>

One more writer of note was produced by the African Church of this age.[1] Arnobius, the teacher of Lactan-

---

[1] Commodianus may be passed over. He wrote two Latin poems c. A.D. 250; but it is not quite certain that he was an African, and his verses are of value chiefly as illustrating the passage of Latin into the Romance languages of the middle ages. He tells us little Church history.

tius, was a rhetorician of Sicca. He was an ardent pagan and public opponent of Christianity. The martyrdoms which he witnessed in the Diocletian persecution converted him, and he applied for baptism. The Christians of Sicca doubted his sincerity, and it is said that in order to convince them he wrote his 'Disputations against the Heathen.' In this treatise he exposes the folly of idolatry, as recently practised by himself, and the unbounded immorality attributed by the heathen themselves to their own gods, especially to Jove. These gods he regards, not as figments, but as evil beings. He is quite at home in pagan mythology; but he never quotes the Old Testament, and the New Testament only once. Yet he knows the life of Christ, and has a lofty conception of God. In a striking passage, which might have found a place in Dr. Mansel's 'Bampton Lectures,' and which may serve as a conclusion to this section, he thus addresses Him: 'O greatest and highest Creator of things invisible, who art Thyself unseen and to all beings incomprehensible! Thou art worthy, Thou art indeed worthy—if mortal tongue may call Thee so—that all that breathes and thinks should never cease to feel and offer thanks to Thee, but all life long fall on bended knee and supplicate in ceaseless prayers. For Thou art the First Cause, the Container of all things, the Foundation of all that is; infinite, unbegotten, immortal, everlasting, alone; whom no bodily form represents, no circuit bounds; in virtue and in greatness undefined; without place, movement, or condition; about whom nothing can be told or expressed by the significance of human words. To understand Thee, we must be silent; and to seek after Thee through the darkness, our wandering conjecture must utter no sound. Grant pardon, King of kings, to those who persecute Thy servants; and according to Thy loving-kindness forgive those who fly from the worship of Thy Name.'

CHAPTER VIII.

THE CHURCHES IN GAUL AND BRITAIN.

AT what time the Gospel was introduced into *Gaul* is quite unknown. There is nothing improbable in this having taken place in the Apostolic age. St. Paul probably went as far as Spain, and Bishop Lightfoot thinks it not improbable that this Western journey included a visit to Gaul. That 'Galatia' to which Crescens went (2 Tim. iv. 10) is Gaul is at least as probable as that it means Asiatic Galatia; and hence the reading Γαλλίαν in Codices ℵ and C as well as in Eusebius. In any case Gaul would not remain long untouched after Italy and Spain had both received Christianity; but the occasion remains uncertain. The legends about Mary Magdalen and the other Maries, and the episcopate of Lazarus for thirty years at Marseilles, may be safely dismissed along with that about Dionysius the Areopagite. No evidence connects the Churches of Gaul with Athens. On the other hand, the connexion between the Church of Lyons and Asia Minor is certain, and we may assume that this Gallican Church was founded by Greek missionaries from Asia Minor. Marseilles was colonised from Asia Minor centuries before

Asiatic origin of the Gallican Church

the Christian era, and its trilingual population spoke Greek side by side with Celtic and Latin. We find Irenæus doing the same. But it is not until his time, not until the second half of the second century, that we get clear evidence of Christianity in Gaul, and then its history bursts on us suddenly with a tragedy. Sulpicius Severus (A.D. 400) tells us that the earliest martyrdoms in Gaul took place under M. Aurelius. This refers primarily to the terrible persecution in A.D. 177, of which we have a vivid though fragmentary account in the priceless letter of the Churches of Lyons and Vienne to the brethren in Asia and Phrygia. A large portion of this letter is preserved by Eusebius, and without much reason some writers have jumped to the conclusion that Irenæus is the author of it. That he is not mentioned in it is in favour of this hypothesis, as also is its moderation. The fanatical tone which disfigures so many narratives of martyrdom is absent. It is its conspicuous simplicity that is so moving; and we should expect this moderation from Irenæus. But Eusebius seems to have no idea that Irenæus wrote it; and he had the whole letter before him. The portion which he quotes shows that two of the sufferers certainly, and a third probably, were natives of Asia Minor—Attalus of Pergamum, Alexander, a physician from Phrygia, and Pothinus, bishop of Lyons. Pothinus was over ninety in A.D. 177, and therefore as a child may have seen St. John. He is likely to have conversed with men who had known the Apostle. These considerations are of importance in the history of the Canon. Pothinus must have known whether the four Gospels and other Apostolic writings had been extant all his life or had come into circulation within his recollection. With Pothinus Irenæus lived in closest intercourse for years; and, although Pothinus has left no writings, we may assume him as one of the witnesses for much that Irenæus states. Indeed, it is probable that Irenæus definitely quotes him as 'the elder.' This elder had 'listened to those who had seen the Apostles,' and Irenæus was evidently very intimate with him. If he was not Pothinus, then he makes a second link between Irenæus and the Apostolic age. Another and still more certain link is found in Polycarp, the teacher of Irenæus and pupil of St. John. Irenæus (c. A.D. 190) writes thus to his fellow-student, the heretically inclined Florinus: 'These views those elders who preceded us, who also were conversant with the Apostles, did not hand down to thee. For I saw thee when I was yet a lad in lower Asia with Polycarp, distinguishing thyself in the royal court, and endeavouring to have his approbation. For I remember what happened then more clearly than recent occurrences. For the experiences of childhood, growing up along with the soul, become part and parcel of it; so that I can describe the very place in which the blessed Polycarp used to sit and discourse, and his goings out and his comings in, the character of his life and the appearance of his person, and the discourses which he used to deliver to the multitude, and how he recounted his close intercourse with John and with the rest of those who had seen the Lord.'

But Asia Minor and Gaul are not the only Churches of which Irenæus is a representative, and to whose traditions he bears witness. Once, certainly, and perhaps more than once, he was for a considerable time in Rome. It is quite possible that he came thither with Polycarp, when the latter paid his visit to Anicetus; and it was almost certainly in Rome that he delivered the lectures on 'All the Heresies' which Hippolytus attended. He took a leading part in the three great controversies of his day—Montanism, the Paschal question, and Gnosticism—in all of which his connexion with the Apostolic age, and with Churches in the East, West, and centre of Christendom, gave him great advantages. Nor does his value as a witness end here. He was evidently a man of education and ability. He was acquainted with a good deal of heathen literature, although he makes little use of his knowledge; for, unlike his contemporary Clement, he disapproved of pagan philosophy. He wrote on various subjects; and the one work which has come down to us shows great research, careful arrangement, and sometimes much acuteness. The 'Refutation and Overthrow of Knowledge falsely so called' is of inestimable value for many reasons, especially for the evidence which it supplies respecting the Canon. Much of it, and perhaps all of it, was written before A.D. 190, and it bears the strongest testimony to the authority of the four Gospels, the Acts, St. Paul's Epistles, some of the Catholic Epistles, and Revelation. And this evidence covers at least fifty years before 190. Irenæus does not know of a time when these books were not accepted as Scripture equal in authority to the books of the Old Testament. It is the earliest Christian work in which evidence of this kind could be expected; and here it is ample and explicit. In letters such as those of Polycarp and Ignatius, or allegories like 'The Shepherd' of

Hermas, or narratives like the story of the martyrs in Gaul, or apologies addressed to Jews and heathen, definite appeals to Christian documents would have been out of place. The wonder is that they contain as much evidence as is found in them. But Irenæus writes to preserve Christians from perversions of the Christian faith, and citations from Christian authorities become natural. They are given in abundance, and frequently with both the writing and the writer named. In interpreting Scripture he lays down some excellent rules, which, however, he does not always keep. The interpretation handed down from the Apostles through the bishops is to be sought for. Difficult passages are not to be explained by hypotheses more difficult still, but by what is clear and consistent. Texts are not to be torn from their context and fitted on to utterly foreign subjects. Still less are disconnected texts to be strung together and made to prove points with which they have nothing to do. All this is like weaving ropes of sand.

Of his private life we know but little. Certainly he was a presbyter of Lyons at the time of the persecution, and after the martyrdom of Pothinus became bishop of that Church. In the interval he went to Rome to intercede with Bishop Eleutherus for the Montanists of Asia Minor on behalf of the confessors in Gaul, who wrote both to Eleutherus and also to the brethren in Asia and Phrygia. All this solicitude of Christians in Gaul for those in Asia Minor proves an intimate connexion between these Churches. Irenæus was bishop of Lyons from c. A.D. 180 to 202, and it is quite possible that at

Growth of the Gallican Church

that time he was the only bishop in Gaul, just as until c. A.D. 200 the bishop of Alexandria was the only bishop in Egypt. The account of the persecution mentions no bishop of Vienne, and Eusebius writes of Irenæus as having more than one diocese, and almost as if he were the only Gallican bishop. His services in protesting against Victor's treatment of the Asiatic Churches, and thus preventing a schism, have been already noticed (pp. 37, 96). But in 250, according to Gregory of Tours (c. A.D. 580), seven bishops were ordained and sent into Gaul to preach; Gatian at Tours, Trophimus at Arles, Paul at Narbonne, Saturninus at Toulouse, Dionysius at Paris (two centuries later than the Areopagite), Stremonius in Auvergne, and Martial at Limoges. The number, seven, is highly suspicious, and the simultaneous founding of all these Churches is improbable. Gregory quotes as his authority the Acts of the Martyrdom of Saturninus, from which he got the date A.D. 250; but that all these other missions took place in the same year is his unsupported assertion. They were probably spread over a considerable period. Later writers add that these missionaries were ordained by the bishop of Rome and sent from Rome to Gaul; but neither the Acts nor Gregory mention Rome or its bishop in connexion with the missions. In any case we may infer from this meagre evidence that the progress of Christianity in Gaul even in the third century was somewhat slow.

We catch another glimpse of Gallican Christianity in connexion with the Novatian schism. Marcianus, bishop of Arles, joined Novatian; and when Faustinus of Lyons and other bishops wrote

Novatianism in Gaul

to Stephen, bishop of Rome, about this scandal, he made no reply. Faustinus then wrote to Cyprian, and Cyprian told Stephen rather plainly that he was neglecting his duty in not helping a neighbouring Church in its distress. 'For this end, my brother, the great body of bishops is united together by the bond of concord and the chain of unity, that if any of our college attempts to promote a heresy and to tear and waste the body of Christ, the rest may come to give help, and, like efficient and compassionate pastors, may gather together the flock of the Lord.' We have no evidence as to how the matter ended.

The great persecution with which the history of the Gallican Church begins in A.D. 177 remains the chief event in its history during the second and third centuries. It was not, however, the only persecution. How much truth there is in the story of the martyrdom of Semphorian at Autun, under Severus, we cannot say. If the Acts of Saturninus may be trusted as to the date 250, Saturninus suffered in the Decian persecution at Toulouse. The Church in Gaul suffered severely under the ruthless Maximian, whose lieutenant Dacian worked much havoc among the Christians of Aquitania, A.D. 286-292. But in 292 Constantius Chlorus, the excellent father of Constantine, was made Cæsar by Diocletian and Maximian, and on their abdication in 305 he became Augustus. Under his good government better times for the Gallican Church began. Both pagans and Christians praise him, and Theophanes of Byzantium (A.D. 800) calls him a man of Christian temper. He received Gaul, Britain, and perhaps Spain as his share of the Empire.

The Menian Schools at Autun—at that time one of the chief educational centres in Europe—were re-established by him. When the last persecution broke out in 303, he did as little as he could in carrying out the edicts, and that little unwillingly. He asked those of his officers who were Christians what they proposed to do. Some said that it would be very painful to them to sacrifice, but that they would do so rather than disobey orders. Others said that it would be most painful to displease him, but that on no account could they sacrifice. He dismissed them without a word; but it was noticed that those who refused to offer incense were those who afterwards received promotion. He told intimate friends that he placed no trust in men who professed fidelity to a heavenly Master, and then betrayed Him in order to profess fidelity to an earthly one. In carrying into effect the orders of Diocletian he allowed the walls of certain churches to be pulled down; 'but the true temple of God, which is in man, he preserved unharmed.' During his reign the number of bishops in Gaul increased to over twenty. He died at York, July 306, naming Constantine as his successor.

Constantine's rule at Treves cannot have been very helpful to Christianity. He built temples and a large amphitheatre, in which he glutted wild beasts with multitudes of unfortunate Franks; and this barbarity he seems to have continued after his return thither in 313 as a professed disciple of Christianity. But the Christian legislation for the Empire which Constantine initiated during the remainder of his life at last made all such things illegal. We take leave of the Church in Gaul just before he issues his orders for the Council

Influence of Constantine

at Arles to put an end to the controversies which 'give occasion of mockery to those who have their minds alienated from the most holy religion.'

We conclude our sketch of the progress of Christianity in the Empire with a glance at *Britain*. Only vague and uncertain evidence is to be obtained respecting this early period; but such as there is must be indicated.

The Church in Britain

The Apostolic origin of the British Church, whether through St. Paul or one of the Twelve, is unproved and improbable.[1] When Eusebius, following Origen, sketches the fields of Apostolic missionary work, he omits Britain ('H. E.' iii. 1).[2] The attractive story of Joseph of Arimathea founding Glastonbury is a mediæval legend of even later date than that of St. James at Compostella in Spain. We have something a little more substantial when Tertullian, among the nations in which the faith has found a home, mentions *Hispaniarum omnes termini, et Galliarum diversæ nationes, et Britannorum inaccessa Romanis loca Christo vero subdita* ('Adv. Jud.' vii.) But an oratorical flourish of this kind need not mean more than that Tertullian knew that the Gospel had spread widely, and liked to give telling details. Irenæus (I. x. 2), writing a little earlier than Tertullian, mentions Germany, Iberia, and the Celts, but says nothing about Britain; and it is quite possible that in his time Christianity had not yet reached our shores.

not founded by an Apostle

[1] Sophronius, patriarch of Jerusalem, A.D. 629, is the very earliest authority for St. Paul's visit to Britain.
[2] The rhetorical passage in *Dem. Ev.* III. iii. p. 112, about 'others crossing the ocean to the islands called British,' leaves us quite in doubt as to who these 'others' are.

But the very circumstantial narrative given by Bede ('H. E.' I. iv.) requires notice. 'In the hundred and fifty-sixth year from the Incarnation of the Lord, Marcus Antoninus Verus, the fourteenth from Augustus, succeeded to the Empire with his brother Aurelius Commodus. In whose time, whilst Eleutherus, a holy man, was bishop of the Roman Church, Lucius, king of Britain, sent a letter to him, entreating that by his command he might be made a Christian; and the fulfilment of his pious request soon followed. And the Britons embraced the faith, and preserved it inviolate and entire in peaceful tranquillity until the time of the Emperor Diocletian.' Thus Bede writes c. A.D. 725. Nennius, c. A.D. 850, gives the story a Welsh turn, and states that 'A.D. 164 Lucius, the British king, with all the chieftains (*reguli*) of the whole of Britain, received baptism, in consequence of a mission sent by the Emperors of the Romans and by the Roman Pope Evaristus.' Three centuries later the imaginative Geoffrey of Monmouth gives the pedigree of Lucius, the names of the missionaries, and other wonderful details. It was the fame of miracles which moved Lucius to send to Rome; and when the holy doctors Faganus and Duvanus arrived, he and multitudes from all countries were baptized. Temples were turned into churches, flamens into bishops, archflamens into archbishops, &c. Evidently Nennius, Geoffrey, and others merely reproduce Bede with variations and additions of their own. What was Bede's source of information? The story is not in Gildas (c. 550) nor in Orosius (c. 430); these are Bede's chief authorities in this early part of his history. Hadden and Stubbs have shown that the story comes from the 'Catalogus Felicianus,' which is a later (c. 530) and interpolated edition of the 'Liberian Catalogue' (c. 354). The original Catalogue gives the bishop's name with the length of his episcopate. The later edition adds, *Hic accepit epistolam a Lucio Britanniæ Rege ut Christianus efficeretur per ejus mandatum*. This, therefore, is the small residuum of history that can be extracted. Eleutherus lived towards the close of the *second* century. In the *sixth* a faint story of a British king seeking Christianity is in existence in Rome, and is connected with Eleutherus. Bede repeats this in somewhat fuller language, and later writers embellish it at pleasure.

Of course a king of all Britain in the second century is impossible. But the story may contain some fragment of truth, such as may underlie the boastful statement of Tertullian. On the other hand, such a story would be likely to be fabricated in Rome in the fifth or sixth century, in order to show that the British Church owed its origin to the Roman see. Similar fabrications, with a similar object, abound. All that we can safely assert, as Hadden and Stubbs have shown, is that there is some reason for believing that there were Christians in Britain before A.D. 200. Certainly there was a British Church with bishops of its own soon after A.D. 300, and possibly some time before that.

probably a fabrication

Very little can be known about this Celtic Church; but the scanty evidence tends to establish three points. (1) It had its origin from, and remained largely dependent upon, the Gallic Church. (2) It was confined almost exclusively to Roman settle-

The British Church

THE CHURCHES IN GAUL AND BRITAIN 141

ments. (3) Its numbers were small and its members were poor.

(1) That Britain should derive its Christianity from Gaul is a highly probable hypothesis. It is confirmed <small>related to Gaul,</small> by the relations between the two Churches. The British Church is frequently drawing on the Gallic. Morgan, better known as the heretic Pelagius, is the one famous person whom the British Church produced, and he lived and studied abroad. When Pelagianism began to spread in Britain, the native teachers were unable to cope with it, and had to send to Gaul for help. When St. Ninias undertook his mission beyond the Forth A.D. 401, it was in connexion with the Gallic bishop St. Martin. St. Patrick's mission to Ireland c. A.D. 440 was also in connexion with Gaul. The saints to whom sacred buildings were commonly dedicated in Britain—Martin, Hilary, and Germain—are Gallic. We know of only one Christian writer in Britain, the semi-Pelagian bishop Fastidius. Gennadius (c. 480), himself of similar views, praises his *sana et digna doctrina*. That Britain may have derived its Christianity from Asia Minor cannot be denied; but the peculiar British custom respecting Easter must not be quoted in evidence of it. It seems to have been a mere blunder, and not a continuation of the old Quartadeciman practice. Gaul is the more probable parent of the British Church.

(2) The sees of the three British bishops at the Council of Arles (314) are Roman headquarters and <small>confined to Roman settlements,</small> probably the capitals of the Roman provinces. The names of the British martyrs Albanus and Julius are Roman. Greek names which occur in

the martyrologies are probably those of Roman slaves or freedmen. Antiquarian traces of British Christianity are very uncommon; but they have been found at places known to have been Roman stations—Canterbury, Dover, Richborough, and Porchester. While Roman remains abound in England, articles distinctly Christian and of the period of Roman occupation are very rare treasures. And this leads us on to the third point.

(3) The fact that very scanty remains of British Christianity survive indicates that British Christians were neither numerous nor wealthy. They had few buildings, and their buildings were not substantial. Their churches were at first of wattlework and earth; then of timber; and at last of stone But when stone buildings began to be erected, the British Church had been driven into the western half of the island, and the English Church—newly born among the heathen invaders—was rapidly taking its place. At the Council of Rimini in 359 Constantius offered to pay out of the treasury the travelling expenses of all the bishops who attended. Out of more than four hundred bishops, three from Britain were the only clergy who availed themselves of this offer. Neither at Rimini, any more than at Arles, do the British representatives make any show: they appear to be quite without influence. It was this insignificance of the British Church which helped to save it from persecution. The martyrdoms of St. Alban and others, if not mere fictions, are transitory exceptions. So far as their isolated position allowed them, the British clergy adopted and maintained the traditions of the Western Churches. Their peculiar customs in the matter of the tonsure and

small and poor

the Easter Cycle, and their peculiar Latin Version of the Bible, were probably mere accidental results of their isolation. They neither derived them from other Churches, nor deliberately adopted them in opposition to other Churches. There is not much evidence of strength or originality anywhere. How soon the demoralisation—painted in such strong colours by Gildas and Bede—began, it is impossible to say; but in the fifth century the clergy are said to have taken the lead in vice. The general orthodoxy of the British Church in the fourth century is attested by Athanasius, Chrysostom, and Jerome.

It seems right to add a word of caution against the common confusion between the British Church and the English Church. They were quite distinct, and had very little to do with one another. To cite the British bishops at the Councils of Arles and Rimini as evidence of the antiquity of the English Church is preposterous. There was then no England; and the ancestors of English Churchmen were heathen tribes on the continent. The history of the Church of England begins with the episcopate of Archbishop Theodore (A.D. 668), or at the very earliest with the landing of Augustine (A.D. 597). By that time the British Church had been almost destroyed by the heathen English, and the remnant of it refused to assist Augustine in the work of conversion. The Scottish Church of Ireland and West Scotland rendered much help: the British Church stood aloof. Bede tells us that down to his day the Britons still treated English Christians as pagans.

The British Church distinct from the English

CHAPTER IX.

LITERARY CONTESTS WITH JEWS AND HEATHEN.

THUS far we have been watching the progress of Christianity in the Roman Empire from its original home in Jerusalem to Gaul and Britain. It has in the main been a chronicle of successes. It remains to point out some of the chief hindrances which the Gospel had to overcome. These were mainly of two kinds—the false accusations made against Christians, and the unjust treatment to which they were subjected. The accusations and the way in which they were met, and the protests against the unjust treatment, are the subject of the present chapter.

Hindrances to Christianity

The charges against Christians were made in various ways. Very often they were mere vulgar prejudices and rumours, arising out of a spirit of hostility which was ready to believe anything bad or suspicious about those whom it disliked. Sometimes they were definite accusations made by literary controversialists. Both these led to formal charges being brought against Christians in the law-courts. Although the patience with which Christians endured ill-treatment made them a byword for 'stubbornness,' yet they did not remain silent under these accumulations of calumnies. As soon as literary men became converted or were reared up in the Church, they began to turn their ability to account in defending the faith and the faithful from attack. Most of these apologists, as we might expect, were converts. They knew both sides

Accusations by the heathen

from personal experience, and had tested in their own lives the value both of what they had abandoned and of what they had gained. Their work extended over more than the whole period that we are considering. From the second to the fifth centuries is the age of the apologists. It culminates in the 'De Civitate Dei' of St. Augustine.

With the apologies the secular or classical literature of the Church begins. Hitherto Christians had avoided styles of writing utterly unlike the Scriptures and closely associated with heathenism. But as they gained confidence they ventured into forms of writing derived from pagan models. Patristic literature is classical literature under Biblical and Christian influences. In less than three centuries from the death of St. John, the Church had appropriated every form of literature known to paganism—the apology, the allegory, the dialogue, the romance, the history, the essay, the oration, the commentary, the hymn, the didactic poem. In this gradual appropriation the apologies led the way. And it is something more than a coincidence that during the process of appropriation classical literature died out. It came to an end in the fifth century, drained of its life-springs by the Christian Church.

Secular literature of the Church

The earlier apologies are defences not so much of Christianity as of Christians. They aim less at proving the truth of the Gospel than at showing that its adherents are neither grossly immoral, nor unpatriotic, nor idle and useless. They claim, not so much that Christianity should be accepted as the one true creed, as that those who do accept it should not be

Early apologies

treated as criminals; and, if accused as criminals, should not be subjected to treatment such as no other accused persons had to endure. They are pleas for toleration and fairness; deprecations of vexatious interference and exceptional treatment.

The apologists did not content themselves with acting on the defensive; it would have been scarcely possible to do so. They carried the war into their opponents' camp by exposing the absurdities and immoralities of paganism, about which they could often speak from personal knowledge. They showed the inconsistency in men with such a creed and such practices persecuting Christians for superstition and impurity, and the injustice of men whose share in foul and cruel rites was never denied punishing others for a worship whose purity had never been disproved. The plea thus became a double one. It contended, first, that the Christians were not only innocent, but estimable; secondly, that, even if they were guilty, their opponents were the people who had the least right to condemn them.

<small>Counter-accusations against paganism</small>

The apologists may be classified in various ways; according to their date, the persons they address, the opponents they answer, and the language they employ. The two last are the most important considerations. There are apologists who answer Jews and who answer heathen. And there are those who write in Greek and who write in Latin. The classification according to date is interesting, chiefly as showing the difference of attitude which time has brought both to the Christian and also to his opponents, and the change in the objections and charges on which most

<small>Classification of the apologists</small>

stress is laid. It is also of interest to note whether the appeal is addressed to an Emperor or civil governor, to a private individual or to the public at large. But neither the date nor the persons addressed affect the apologies so much as the influences which are connected with the opponents who are answered, and the language which is employed in the reply. Yet, as a matter of fact, the division according to language to a large extent corresponds with that according to time. The apologists of the second century are mainly Greek; those of the third mainly Latin.

It is obvious that an answer to a Jew must differ a good deal from an answer to a pagan; it is not so Greek and obvious that an apology in Latin is likely to Latin apologists differ from an apology in Greek. Yet the difference between the two may be called fundamental. It is the difference which is summed up in the contrast between Roman law and Greek thought. The instruments of the Greek apologists were reason and philosophy; those of the Latin were rhetoric and law. The broad characteristics which distinguish Greek and Latin literature reappear here. In the one case the appeal is to what is universal, to the high aspirations and deep thoughts which the human mind in its freedom has anywhere reached. It is the Gospel, rather than Judaism or heathenism, that sums up and satisfies all these. In the other case the appeal is to the rights of the individual, to social order, to common sense, and to law.

The destruction of Jerusalem severed Christianity The contro- from Judaism; the suppression of the Jewish versy with Judaism revolt under Barcochba turned the severed parties into opponents. Henceforward the Jewish

Christian in the eyes of the Jew was not merely a rival but a traitor, and the Gentile Christian was one who enjoyed the gains of treason at the Jew's expense. The animosity was intense; and to abuse the Christians, or to stir up the heathen to persecute them, was a delight, if not a duty, to a Jew. Constantly in the persecutions we find the Jews prominent in the attack. There were literary attacks also on the Jewish side, and these had to be met with the pen. The miraculous birth and the Divinity of Christ had to be maintained against denials and foul insinuations. The spiritual meaning of types and prophecies, and the superseding of the Law by the Gospel, had to be explained. Christians had to make good their claim to be the true Israel of God. Of extant Greek writings of this type the chief are the so-called 'Epistle of Barnabas' (c. A.D. 80-110), Justin Martyr's 'Dialogue with Trypho' (c. A.D. 155), the 'Demonstratio adversus Judæos' of Hippolytus (c. A.D. 220), and parts of Origen's 'Contra Celsum' (A.D. 249). We know also of a 'Discussion about Christ between Jason and Papiscus,' sometimes attributed to Ariston of Pella; but it is lost. Celsus ridiculed it; but Origen speaks of it with respect, as showing in answer to Jewish arguments that the prophecies respecting the Messiah were fulfilled in Jesus. Latin writings against Jews are less numerous. There is the 'Adversus Judæos' of Tertullian, and the 'Testimonia adversus Judæos' of Cyprian. The latter is a large selection of texts skilfully arranged. Its value in determining the text of the Latin Versions in use in Africa is immense. There is also the 'Epistola de Cibis Judaicis' of Novatian to prove that Christian principles of temperance have superseded Jewish restrictions upon food.

The Jews had two main arguments against Christianity. (1) The mean life and ignominious death of Jesus contradict the prophecies about the glories of the Messiah. (2) The Divinity of Jesus is blasphemy and contradicts the Divine Unity. To these it was replied that both types and prophecies indicate that the Christ is to suffer as well as reign, and that a plurality of Persons in the Godhead is taught in the Old Testament along with the Divine Sonship of the Christ. When Judaism had to be attacked as well as answered, the destruction of Jerusalem was a powerful argument. To keep the Law was no longer possible.

But the bulk of the apologies are directed against heathenism. The earliest known to us are those of the Athenians Quadratus and Aristides, addressed to Hadrian. Hadrian's *dilettante* curiosity and studied good-nature encouraged people to send him philosophic statements respecting the merits of an interesting cult. With his predecessors such attempts would have had no success. A fragment of the work of Quadratus is preserved by Eusebius, and is an important item in the evidence for miracles. Just as St. Paul appeals to the hundreds of people still living who had seen the risen Christ, so Quadratus appeals to the long lives of many who had been healed by Christ. 'Some of them lived even into our own times.' A fragment of what is believed by some to be an Armenian translation of the 'Apology' of Aristides has recently been discovered. If so, it is one more witness to the belief of primitive Christendom in the incarnation, resurrec-

The controversy with paganism

tion, and ascension. It divides mankind into barbarians, Greeks, Jews, and Christians. But the earliest *extant* apologies are those of Justin Martyr, addressed (c. A.D. 140 and 155) to Antoninus Pius. The 'Embassy' of Athenagoras and the 'Apology' of Melito, Bishop of Sardis, were addressed (c. A.D. 177) to M. Aurelius; and to the same reign belong the 'Oratio ad Græcos' of Tatian, the 'Apology' of Claudius Apollinaris, and the 'Ad Autolycum' of Theophilus, with perhaps the 'Cohortatio ad Græcos,' sometimes ascribed to Justin. Near the end of the second century we have the 'Liber Adhortatorius ad Græcos' of Clement of Alexandria and the 'Irrisio Gentilium Philosophorum' of Hermias. The great work of Origen, 'Contra Celsum,' was published A.D. 249. The Latin treatises against paganism probably begin with the 'Octavius' of Minucius Felix, c. A.D. 160; but some critics place this finished little work later. Then comes the 'Apologeticus adversus Nationes' of Tertullian, c. 200, with his shorter 'Ad Nationes' and 'Ad Scapulam.' In 246 Cyprian wrote 'Ad Demetrianum.'

The heathen objections to Christianity were numerous. Some of them might have been urged against other religions; it was the combination of them all which seemed so monstrous in Christianity. (1) It was a novel religion, and therefore untrue. (2) Its alleged miracles were incredible. (3) Still more incredible was its leading doctrine of the resurrection of the body. (4) It was a religion of ignorant fanatics. (5) The Christians were joyless, useless members of society, and unpatriotic citizens. (6) They were a secret society. (7) They were atheists; for they

The pagan attack

had no images of the gods and no temples. (8) In insulting the worship of all recognised deities they were guilty of sacrilege. (9) In refusing to sacrifice to the Emperor they were guilty of high treason. (10) They practised magic. (11) They were grossly immoral; for they had 'love-feasts,' which were incestuous orgies, and 'sacred mysteries,' in which they partook of human flesh and blood. (12) The frequent famines, locusts, earthquakes, wars, and pestilences were judgments on mankind for tolerating such miscreants. This last was the cry of the mob; and from A.D. 100 to 250 it often drove officials to persecute who would otherwise have been tolerant. During this period the masses, in their ignorance of Christian rites and morals, commonly took the lead in persecutions.

All these charges are met by the apologists. (1) The Gospel is not new; it has its roots in Paradise at the birth of the human race. Moses is far more ancient than any pagan writer. (2) Miracles cannot be incredible when paganism itself claims to have them. Christian miracles are guaranteed by their publicity, their effects, and the good faith of the witnesses. (3) If God is omnipotent, resurrection must at least be possible; the close connexion of soul and body renders it probable, and this probability is increased by numerous analogies in nature. (4) Philosophers and scholars had not only become Christians, but remained such. In any large society the ignorant always outnumber the instructed. (5) Christians were the happiest and most contented of men, devoted to the well-being of others, and ready to die for the State. They kept aloof from many heathen pleasures, not

The Christian reply, both defensive

because they were pleasures, but because they were sinful. There were certain services which they could not, without sin, render to the State. (6) Their secresy was a matter not of choice but of necessity. So long as they were persecuted, self-preservation compelled them to conceal their religion. (7) They worshipped a God who is spirit, and dwells not in temples made with hands. (8) There was no sacrilege in despising the worship of those who were no gods. (9) To offer sacrifice to a mortal was blasphemous folly. (10) Magic was forbidden among them. Their sacred books contained no charms or spells. Demons were cast out, not by any unlawful means, but in the name of Jesus Christ. (11) So far from countenancing incest, Christians forbad all impurity, even in thought. So far from being cannibals, they condemned all bloodshed, even such as was commonly tolerated, as infanticide and gladiatorial contests. The 'kiss of peace' was a pure and holy salutation; and they were all 'brothers' and 'sisters' as being children of God, not as the result of unnatural unions. (12) If the calamities falling on mankind were judgments, they were judgments on those who rejected the true God and worshipped devils. But the world was growing old and its forces were worn out. Christians were no more responsible for bad seasons than they were for old age and decay.

From this it was easy to pass on and attack paganism for its own follies and enormities. Here heathen philosophers had already led the way in showing *and offensive* that a plurality of gods was an absurdity, and gods with human passions and vices a degrading absurdity. And what the philosophers disproved, the comic poets held up to ridicule. Nor was either party reproved. From Nero to Diocletian there is no instance of a philosopher being prosecuted for freethinking, or a poet for impiety. As the Christians pointed out, to insult a man was a punishable offence, but any one might vilify the gods. The gods continued to be worshipped—that is, sacrifices were offered to them as a matter of State ritual, or in order to bribe them to help in some crime. But no one reverenced them. The images in which they were supposed to dwell were frequently made of loathsome materials and treated with the utmost indignity. And what a history these gods have! There is no mean, false, cruel, or foul act that has not been attributed to them. They are not gods, but devils. Hence, although Christians agree with the philosophers in rejecting such deities, and with the poets in deriding them, yet they cannot admit that to offer sacrifice to them is a meaningless and harmless act. To worship a nonentity would be a profanation of worship; but the worship of these divinities is worse than that—it is the worship of demons. In any case it is an act of treason to the true God and His Christ. Worship implies the inferiority of the worshipper; and the faith of the humblest Christian can put to flight any of these devils. 'By their fruits ye shall know them.' Contrast the pure and benevolent lives of Christians with the shameless, self-seeking lives of their opponents. Who is it that controls his passions, that cherishes his kindred, that takes care of the stranger, that succours his enemy, that shrinks not from death?

With the philosophers apologists had to take a somewhat different line. Pagan wisdom had demolished

polytheism, but had put nothing in its place. In the attempt to reconstruct they had failed; and they admitted
<small>The reply to</small> their failure. Popular mythology was cer-
<small>heathen philosophy</small> tainly false, but it was impossible to determine
what was true. Perhaps there was a God. Perhaps there was a future state. Philosophy could neither affirm nor deny. Was it possible to regenerate mankind with this gospel of uncertainties? The teachers of it could not regenerate themselves. In public they reviled one another, and in private led vicious lives. They might sharpen the intellects of men; but they could neither curb their passions, nor touch their hearts, nor control their wills. And here the Greek and the Latin apologists parted company. Both proclaimed the insufficiency and failure of philosophy; but the Greeks did so with sympathy, the Latins with contempt. The Greek apologists for the most part
<small>by Greeks</small> allowed that heathen philosophy contained precious elements of truth, which sometimes were direct inspirations of the Divine Word, sometimes were borrowed from the Jewish Scriptures. These elements had prepared the way for something better. The chief exceptions to this way of thinking are Irenæus, who had no sympathy with Greek speculation, Tatian, who condemned it, and Hermias, who ridiculed it. These three were more in harmony with the Latin apolo-
<small>by Latins</small> gists, who for the most part regarded pagan philosophy as a mere obstacle, which must be removed to make way for the Gospel. In Tatian this view marks the Asiatic's dislike of everything Greek, a feeling in which Africans also shared. In this gloomy and vehement Assyrian there is much that reminds us

of Tertullian. Tertullian thinks that philosophers are 'blockheads when they knock at the doors of truth,' and that 'they have contributed nothing whatever that a Christian can accept.' Arnobius says that, 'by bringing to nought one another's doctrines, they have made all things doubtful, and by their want of agreement have proved that nothing can be known.' Lactantius denies that philosophy is even so much as the pursuit of wisdom; for 'if this pursuit were a kind of road to wisdom, wisdom would at length be found.' Philosophers imagine themselves to be seeking truth, 'because they know not where that is which they are seeking for, nor what its nature is.' They testify to the unity of God after a fashion, but they are like disinherited sons who do not seek their father, or runaway slaves who avoid their master. They know not that God is Father and Lord of all. Just as the worship of the gods is false religion, so the guesswork of the philosophers is false wisdom.

The apologists were not content with defending Christianity against attack and attacking Judaism and paganism in return. They also endeavoured to set forth the reasonableness of Christianity and the arguments in its favour. Among these arguments *prophecies* and *types* held a very prominent place. God alone can foresee the distant future and cause the present to be prefigured in the past. Therefore a religion, which has been so abundantly foretold and typified from the very earliest ages, must be divine. In working out the details of this argument they sometimes went to extravagant lengths. The Old Testament was made to be very elastic in order to exhibit it throughout

The arguments from prophecy

as an anticipation of the Gospel; and the so-called Sibylline oracles, without any enquiry into their origin, were treated in a similar way. In the same uncritical spirit a work which was really of Christian authorship, 'The Testaments of the Twelve Patriarchs,' was treated as a detailed prophecy of the lives of Christ and St. Paul. But when all deductions for these mistakes have been made, the argument remains a solid one. The Old Testament cannot reasonably be explained without admitting a strong prophetic element, and even in pagan literature there is a yearning and a hope for the better things in store for mankind which may fairly be called an 'unconscious presentiment' of Christianity.

The appeal to *miracles* was less frequently made. In an age in which every one believed in magic this argument was not a very serviceable one, unless combined with another—viz. the *moral purpose and effect* of the Gospel. When did a magician ever make any one more virtuous, or even attempt to do so? His wonders were wrought to gain applause or money, not to bring men nearer to God. The lives of these wonder-workers were commonly scandalous, whereas both by example and precept the preachers of Christianity taught men to love virtue and to reverence God. The contrast both in aim and in result between pagan and Christian teaching is a frequent and fruitful argument. Every one who is acquainted with the classical literature of the first two centuries knows the moral gulf which separated the ordinary heathen from the ordinary Christian. The contrast is beautifully drawn out on the Christian side in the 'Epistle to

Diognetus.' 'It is neither by country, nor by language, nor by fashions, that Christians are distinguished from the rest of mankind. . . . They dwell in their native land, but as sojourners. They take part in all things as citizens, and endure all things as strangers. Every foreign land is fatherland to them, and every fatherland is foreign. They marry, as all do, and beget children; but they do not cast away their offspring. They have a common table, but not a common bed. They are in the flesh; but they do not live after the flesh. They pass their days upon the earth; but they are citizens of heaven. They obey prescribed laws; and by their own lives excel the laws. They love all; and are persecuted by all. Men know them not; 'and men condemn them . . . and the reason for their enmity those who hate them cannot tell. In a word, what soul is in body, Christians are in the world. The soul is diffused through all the limbs of the body, and Christians through the cities of the world. The soul dwells in the body, but it is not of the body; and Christians dwell in the world, but are not of the world. The invisible soul keeps watch in the visible body; and Christians are known to be in the world, but their godliness remains invisible. The flesh hates the soul and wars against it, not as being wronged, but because it is checked in its fill of pleasures; and the world hates Christians, not as being wronged, but because they oppose its pleasures. The soul loves the flesh that hates it; and Christians love those that hate them. The soul is shut up in the body; but it keeps the body from dissolution: and Christians are kept in the world as in a prison; but they keep the world from dissolution. Immortal itself, the soul dwells in a mortal tabernacle ; and Christians sojourn in what is corruptible, looking for the incorruption that is in heaven. When ill served in meat and drink, the soul is made better; and Christians, when punished day by day, abound more and more. Such is the post in which God has placed them, and it is not lawful for them to refuse it.'

We have little means of estimating the effect produced by the apologists. Jerome asserts that Quadratus and Aristides were among the influences which induced Hadrian to publish the rescript to Minucius Fundanus which stands at the end of the second 'Apology' of Justin. This document gives the Christians no more than Trajan had given in his directions to Pliny, except that it imposes severe penalties on false accusers. Nevertheless we know of only one martyrdom —that of Telesphorus—which certainly took place in this reign, and only a few more which can reasonably be assigned to it. Therefore the result of the rescript was favourable ; and Melito tells us that several orders of similar import were sent by Hadrian to the provinces. That Antoninus Pius was persuaded by Justin's 'Apology' to put a stop to persecution is a very questionable statement. The decree given by Eusebius ('H. E.' IV. xiii.), and appended in a different form to Justin's first 'Apology,' is now generally condemned as spurious. On the other hand, it is by no means improbable that the 'Apologeticus' of Tertullian had something to do with provoking the edict of Septimius Severus which made conversion to Christianity penal. So scathing an exposure of pagan vice, folly, and injustice must have been most exasperating to Roman officials. But, if the apologies had

Results of the apologies

little effect on Emperors and governors (and perhaps in some cases never reached them), they influenced public opinion. They set men thinking. Some of the points urged were indisputable; and, whether men liked them or not, they could not ignore them. Even those who never read these treatises heard of the arguments through Christians and others who had studied them, The apologies taught ordinary Christians how to defend themselves and retort on their opponents, and through reiteration the better cause prevailed.

The student who wishes to read typical examples of apologies could hardly do better than select that of Origen 'Against Celsus' on the Greek side, and the 'Apologeticus' of Tertullian on the Latin side. It is a serious mistake to suppose that 'Celsus was not a formidable antagonist.' On the contrary, 'it would be difficult to overrate the importance both of the attack and of the defence in relation to the history of religious opinion in the second and third centuries. The form of objections changes; but it may be said fairly that every essential type of objection to Christianity finds its representative in Celsus's statements, and Origen suggests in reply thoughts, often disguised in strange dresses, which may yet be fruitful. . . . Among early apologies it has no rival. The constant presence of a real antagonist gives unflagging vigour to the debate; and the conscious power of Origen lies in the appeal which he makes to *the Christian life as the one unanswerable proof of the Christian faith.*' The answer to Celsus is one of Origen's later works, written when his great powers were at their best. And we possess it in the original Greek; whereas in the case of some of his writings we have only the garbled and exceedingly untrustworthy translations of Rufinus.

Of Tertullian's defence of Christianity Jerome says, 'What more learned than Tertullian, what more acute? His "Apology" and his books against the Gentiles comprise the whole range of secular learning.' It would be difficult to find a plea on the ground of equity, or of common sense, or of logical and legal consistency, that is not urged by him with point and vigour. But the vigour is overdone, and good arguments are spoiled by being coupled with bad ones. The self-willed vehemence of this primitive Lamennais began by damaging the cause which he defended, and ended in carrying him outside the Church.

CHAPTER X.

THE PERSECUTIONS.

FROM the time of St. Augustine it has been customary to talk of the ' *ten* persecutions'—viz. those under Nero, Domitian, Trajan, Marcus Aurelius, Septimius Severus, Maximin, Decius, Valerian, Aurelian, and Diocletian. Augustine substitutes Antoninus for M. Aurelius. He protests against the view that the ten plagues of Egypt foreshadowed the persecutions; but there is little doubt that the ten plagues suggested the number ten. It would be easy to reduce the number with Lactantius to six, or to increase it considerably. There were not even six persecutions which prevailed throughout the Empire; only those of Decius and Dio-

The number of the persecutions indefinite

cletian did that. And if we count local persecutions, we can find many more than ten. Probably the ten kings making war against the Lamb (Rev. xvii. 14) helped to influence the arrangement. We may adopt Augustine's conclusion, that the precise number cannot be stated.

Humanly speaking, it was inevitable that Christianity should provoke the bitter hostility of both the Jew and the heathen. Of the Jew, because it claimed to supersede the Law and to rob the Chosen People of their privileges by throwing open salvation to all mankind. Of the heathen, because it was an innovation, an *imperium in imperio*, a religion which claimed to be both universal and exclusive, and which condemned and opposed all other religions, including those forms of worship imposed by the State. In the case both of Jew and of Gentile the Gospel had to encounter the conservatism of priests backed up by the conservatism of lawyers. In the case of the Roman government and hierarchy this opposition was intensified by the conviction that the Christian society was not only an innovation, but a dangerous one. Roman jealousy of associations which did not originate with the State is notorious; and here was a huge organisation silently extending itself through every province in the Empire. Its existence was a perpetual menace to civil government. Already its members were coming into collision with Imperial ordinances, and neither remonstrance nor punishment could induce them to give way. They spoke among themselves of a Kingdom to which they belonged, and of a King to whom they owed an allegiance which superseded their obligations to the Emperor. Far-reaching as was the Imperial arm, here was a sphere

The chief causes: conservatism and fear

in which it seemed to be paralysed. It could quell a rebellion in Persia or in Britain, but at the very gates of the palace was a power which baffled it. This power had its officials—often men of no position in the world— who in their own community were more than a match for the Emperor himself. They were his subjects, and he could take their lives. But no sooner was one official executed than another took his place. The man was gone, but the system went on as before. Hostility to the Church, engendered by conservatism and intensified by suspicion, reached a climax when experience proved that neither argument, nor ridicule, nor repressive measures availed to check Christianity. The heathen in their turn became afraid. The persecutions, which began in ignorance and dislike, were continued in hatred and fear. The chief motive of the worst attacks on the Christians was neither wantonness, nor contempt, nor cruelty, but terror. Pagan society felt itself in the meshes of a net, whose steadily increasing extent and strength had baffled all attempts to destroy it. It was this feeling of failure and helplessness against an unknown power which exasperated the masses in the first half of the persecutions and the officials in the second half. Down to about A.D. 250 it was the frenzied populace who stirred up the magistrates against the Christians; after 250 it was commonly the magistrates who stirred up the people. In both cases the heathen were well aware that they had had every advantage on their side—authority, rank, wealth, education, numbers, tradition, physical force. And yet in spite of all these they were not victorious. They had lost much and gained nothing; and they were frantic at the prospect of defeat. There is no cruelty more reckless than that which is born of terror; and it was frenzy of this kind which inspired the savage outcries and diabolical legal proceedings adopted against the Christians.

But it was not merely as innovators, or as members of a mysterious organisation, that Christians were hated and feared; it was also as promoters of a religion which condemned all other religions as false. We are accustomed to think of the Romans as tolerant. And polytheists must to some extent be tolerant, for the gods of other people may be as powerful as their own, and as capable of protecting their worshippers. But the toleration of the Romans had tightly drawn limits. Cicero had laid it down as an axiom that no man may have private gods of his own or adopt fresh ones until they have been officially recognised; and Mæcenas is represented as advising Augustus to worship the gods according to the laws, and *compel others to do the same*— not merely out of respect to the gods, but because those who introduce new deities may go on to introduce new laws. The Christians, therefore, committed a double offence—they induced citizens to abandon the rites prescribed by law, and they introduced rites not sanctioned by law. Theirs was not a *religio licita*. As they were repeatedly told, *Non licet esse vos*—'You have no right to exist.' Had it been content to enter on equal terms with two or three hundred other religions, Christianity might have been tolerated. Its claim to be the one true faith for the whole world was, from the Roman point of view, fatal. It was this which brought Christians into collision with the best of the Roman Emperors. A Commodus or an Elagabalus might care little as to the

[margin note: Limits to Roman toleration]

amount of 'foreign superstition' in which his subjects indulged. But to earnest rulers like Trajan, M. Aurelius, and Decius, it was a matter of conscience to see that the State was obeyed and the State religion respected. The eternity of Rome and its gods was a first principle in Roman politics. It was impossible to allow large bodies of citizens to teach systematically that Rome and the whole Empire would shortly perish, and that the divinities of Rome were demons. The chief pagan charges against Christianity have been already stated (p. 150). Several of these brought Christians within the sweep of long-established laws. And hence the great variety of punishments which magistrates could inflict according to the view which they chose to take of Christianity. It might be treated as an unlicensed religion, or as high treason, or as sacrilege, or as magic; perhaps also as incest. Introducers of new religions, if of good birth, were to be banished to an island; otherwise were to be put to death. Those guilty of high treason, if of good birth, were to be beheaded; if not, to be exposed to the beasts or burned alive. In either case they might be tortured. Sacrilege was similarly punished, with the additional alternative of crucifixion, but with the exclusion of torture in the case of citizens. Magic was punishable with exposure to wild beasts, burning, or crucifixion; incest with banishment. Such a combination of crimes in one and the same set of men naturally made Roman officials intolerant.

The common assignment of the persecutions to ten Emperors is misleading in other ways besides that of assuming numerical exactness where no such exactness is attainable. It seems to assume that the other

THE PERSECUTIONS 165

Emperors did *not* persecute Christianity, which is far from being the case. Some of the omitted Emperors—e.g. Antoninus Pius—were worse persecutors than some of the ten. And in the reigns of all of them down to the Edict of Gallienus (A.D. 261) Christianity remained a *religio illicita*, to be suppressed by any magistrate who cared to interest himself in the matter. Moreover, the common arrangement encourages the idea that the persecutions were all of a similar character, differing chiefly in intensity and duration; whereas there were three distinct kinds, even among the ten enumerated. Those under Nero and Domitian were capricious outbursts of personal cruelty and tyranny. Those under Decius, Valerian, and Diocletian were systematic attempts to extinguish Christianity throughout the Empire. The other five were for the most part fitful enforcements of existing laws with exceptional severity in particular districts The epochs in the struggle are marked by the reigns of Trajan, Decius, Valerian, and Diocletian.

<small>Errors respecting 'the ten persecutions'</small>

Until Trajan's time the Roman government had not stated its attitude towards Christianity. Two circumstances compelled it then to define its position. (1) Since the fall of Jerusalem and the persecution of Christians by Jews, it had become manifest that the followers of Christ were not a Jewish sect. Judaism was a *religio licita*; Christianity, if not a form of Judaism, was not. (2) The increase in the numbers of the Christians made the question a pressing one. It was towards the end of A.D. 112 that Pliny wrote his famous letter to Trajan stating the urgency of the matter in his own province of Bithynia. Strong

<small>Crisis under Trajan</small>

repressive measures had already been tried by him; but the results were unsatisfactory and perplexing. Some, who persisted in professing Christianity when brought before his tribunal, he had sentenced to death. Their inflexible obstinacy seemed to him sufficient crime, whatever might be the nature of Christianity. This it was not easy to determine. From those who had been Christians years ago, and from two deaconesses examined under torture, he had learnt that Christians met together on a stated day before daybreak and sang hymns to Christ as a god, that they bound themselves by an oath not to do anything criminal, but to avoid theft, violence, adultery, lying, and fraud. Then they separated and met again for a meal, which, however, was open to them all and innocent. Even this they had given up on his forbidding clubs and guilds. He had been able to discover nothing worse than a wrong-headed and boundless superstition. Trajan on the whole approves of his friend's proceedings, and gives the following express directions. (1) Christians are not to be sought out; but if formally accused and convicted, they are to be punished. (2) Those who deny that they are Christians and worship 'our gods' are to be pardoned, however suspicious their past history may have been. (3) Anonymous accusations must not be accepted; to receive them would be a precedent of the worst kind, and unworthy of an enlightened age. For the next hundred years these were the principles on which Christians were treated by the State; and the spirit in which the principles were applied in different provinces and at different times made the whole difference between persecution and peace. As a rule, yet by no means invariably, officials took their cue from their superiors; but it was probably easier for an energetic governor to persecute under a tolerant Emperor than for a tolerant governor to hold back when an Imperial edict ordered action.

These opposite results from the same instructions explain the contradictory opinions which the Christians themselves held respecting the action of Trajan. Some regarded him as a protector of the Church; and one of the most famous of mediæval legends represents him as released from hell at the intercession of Pope Gregory I., while another represents Pliny as being converted to Christianity. Others, again, regarded Trajan as one of the worst of the persecutors; and some modern writers have represented him as the first systematic persecutor. But there is no reason for believing that Trajan either consciously or unconsciously initiated a new departure with regard to the Christians. He was perhaps the first to issue permanent orders on the subject; but his orders did not make Christianity illegal. As it had never been sanctioned by the State, it had always been illegal. Trajan's rescript merely emphasised the fact and gave some rules for dealing with it. These rules were generous from the Emperor's point of view. They secured Christians a formal trial and protected them from anonymous delation. In this respect they were to have equal justice with other suspected persons. But the Christians were not to be sought out. In this respect they were treated better than other suspected persons. It was not very logical from the legal point of view, as Tertullian sarcastically points out. 'He forbids their

Its double aspect

being sought out, as if they were innocent; and commands their being punished, as if they were guilty.' But Trajan's object was to do his duty in putting down an illegal sect and suppressing a dangerous society; and he believed the best way to attain his end was to be both firm and conciliatory. No one was to be driven to desperation. Amnesty was to be freely offered to all who would leave the forbidden community. But no mercy was to be shown to those who were publicly accused and convicted.

Although Hadrian has a bad name as a persecutor, yet only one martyrdom can with certainty be assigned to his reign—viz. that of Telesphorus, the first Bishop of Rome of whose martyrdom we have sure knowledge. But it is possible that there were other martyrdoms, especially towards the end of the reign, when Hadrian's mind became affected. Otherwise Hadrian was hardly serious enough to be a persecutor. To be thought agreeable, to be an amateur philosopher, critic, and patron of art and literature, to go through life with the well-bred smile of a cultivated man of the world—these were his aims. To have persecuted would have seemed unamiable, narrow-minded, and in bad taste. The frequent references to persecution in the 'Shepherd' of Hermas probably refer to occurrences in the later days of Hadrian. Jerome, who places the persecutions early in the reign, says that Hadrian put a stop to them in consequence of the apologies presented to him at Athens A.D. 125.

Misconceptions respecting Hadrian

Antoninus Pius, excepting by Augustine, is not reckoned among persecuting Emperors, and his reign is commonly regarded as one of peace for the Christians.

THE PERSECUTIONS 169

Yet it was under him that Publius, Bishop of Athens, and Polycarp, Bishop of Smyrna, with his companions, suffered. Another group of martyrs in this reign illustrates the kind of thing that was always possible under the rules promulgated by Trajan. A wife was accused by her husband of being a Christian. She got the trial postponed; and he then accused Ptolemæus, her instructor. In court Ptolemæus was merely asked, 'Are you a Christian?' He said 'Yes,' and was at once sentenced to death. One Lucius remonstrated with the prefect for condemning a man simply for being a Christian. '*You* also seem to be one,' was the reply; and, on his admitting it, he too was sentenced to death. And then a third came forward and was likewise punished. Justin Martyr, who tells the story, says that he expected to be denounced and condemned himself.

and Antoninus

But Justin's turn to bear witness by his death did not come until the reign of the philosopher-Emperor M. Aurelius. There are few sadder pictures in history than that of the author of the 'Meditations' torturing and slaying, not hastily or fitfully, but deliberately and on principle, the followers of Jesus Christ. The persecutions in this reign are not the work of fanatical governors acting without special orders; they are the Emperor's own work. We can trace them with certainty in Asia Minor, Rome, Gaul, and Africa; and no doubt they took place in many other places. And they continued throughout the whole reign. If Trajan was the first to formulate the principle that it was criminal to be a Christian, M. Aurelius was the first to work the principle thus formulated with

Tragic reign of M. Aurelius

unflinching severity. That he did so from a profound sense of duty no student of his character can doubt. But the tragic irony of such a moral contradiction cannot easily be surpassed. The last and best product of pagan civilisation declares war to the death upon the one society which was capable of carrying out his own noble aspiration of purifying and elevating mankind. Let us excuse his ignorance of Christianity. Ought not his philosophy to have taught him the uselessness, if not the iniquity, of persecution? Ought not statecraft to have warned him against giving enthusiasts the stimulus of martyrdom? Read the account of the martyrdoms at Lyons and Vienne, and remember that they were conducted under the express sanction of the man who wrote, 'Who can change the opinions of men? And without a change of sentiments what can you make but reluctant slaves and hypocrites?' 'Men were made for men. Correct them, then, or endure them'. 'Correct them, if you can. If not, remember that patience was given you to practise for their good.' 'It is against its will that the soul is deprived of virtue. Ever remember this; the thought will make you more gentle to all mankind.' Renan tells us that the gospel of M. Aurelius will never become obsolete, because it affirms no dogma. The latter statement is hardly true, for the Emperor maintains that of a surety there are gods and they care for mankind. A belief in a Providence is the basis of his fortitude. Without this dogma his teaching would be the gospel of suicide. 'What good is it to me,' he asks, 'to live in a world destitute of Providence?' Renan is nearer the truth when he points out that the teaching of M. Aurelius fortifies, but cannot console. Will that gospel never become obsolete which has no consolations to offer to mankind; which inflicts suffering, but does not alleviate it; which makes the adherents of other creeds martyrs, but produces no martyrs of its own? Melito of Sardis, in his apology addressed to M. Aurelius, complains of 'fresh edicts' against the Christians. The chief advance on the policy of Trajan seems to have been the order that informers against the Christians were to receive the property of the condemned. This iniquitous provision almost amounted to a general proscription of Christians throughout the Empire. And the results were hideous. The mines were crowded with prisoners. Torture and bloodshed went on continually in Asia, Byzantium, Africa, and Gaul. In their heart-stirring narrative the Gallican Christians say that they are telling but a portion of the suffering, for to tell the whole would be impossible.

It was far the worst persecution which the Church had thus far experienced, and it did not cease imme-
Toleration under Commodus diately on the Emperor's death (A.D. 180). But Commodus soon put a stop to it: and his accession, however disastrous to the Empire, was a gain to the Church. His promotion of the 'God-loving concubine' Marcia to be Empress in 183 secured peace for the Christians; and for about twenty years the Churches had rest. We know of only one martyrdom during this period. Apollonius, a senator, was denounced by his slave and condemned to death by the Senate c. A.D. 186. On the other hand, Marcia obtained the release of many Christians from the horrors of the mines in Sardinia.

But while Christianity thus gained time for recruiting its forces, heathenism also was doing the same. The calamities of the Empire had frightened mankind. War, pestilence, bad seasons, locusts, famines, and general bankruptcy prevailed. The insulted divinities, it was suspected, were taking vengeance for man's neglect of them. After all there *were* gods with whom mankind must reckon. And thus a boundless scepticism was succeeded by a boundless superstition. Old rites were revived; new rites were invented. Nothing was too monstrous to be done in order to win back the favour, or at least propitiate the wrath, of the powers unseen. Heathen society, after years of godless profligacy, tried to turn religious in its old age; and, in order to retain something of excitement under the change, it devoted its attention chiefly to the fantastic worship of foreign gods and to the mysteries of theurgy and magic. The sober rites of the old Roman deities were to a large extent exchanged for a frenzied demon-worship far more hostile to Christianity both in its own character and in the temper which it generated. Chief among these cults was the worship of the Persian god Mithras, whose statues still abound. Hippolytus has some graphic descriptions of the juggleries practised at these witches' sabbaths; and Lucian gives a detailed exposure of the impostures perpetrated at them in his account of the 'pseudomantis,' Alexander of Abonoteichus. Jaded voluptuaries were gratified by the consecration of nameless indulgences. Terrified consciences were soothed by hideous self-inflicted punishments. The spiritual cravings of more earnest souls were deluded by supposed

Revival of paganism

intercourse with the unseen. It was at this time that Philostratus wrote his life of Apollonius of Tyana, decorated with a profusion of mysteries and miracles to gratify the taste of the age and to outbid Christianity.

Roughly speaking, we may distinguish three influences at work in producing the revival of paganism;—
Nature of the revival philosophy of the Neo-Platonic and Neo-Pythagorean type; Orientalism, especially in the form of sun-worship; and a vague Monotheism, admitting the worship of all deities as symbols of divine attributes. This last is sometimes called Pantheism; but the Supreme Being, though scarcely personal, was not identified with the universe. These three elements of revived heathenism had each of them an Imperial patroness. Julia Domna, wife of Septimius Severus, interested herself in the first and encouraged Philostratus. Her elder niece, Julia Soëmia, mother of Elagabalus, supported the second. Her younger niece, Julia Mammæa, mother of Alexander Severus, favoured the third; and hence, very probably, her interest in so acute and religious a thinker as Origen. But these three influences were not all. There was underneath them something far more real. This religious revival was not merely the result of dismay at existing and impending calamities; it was also the expression of a yearning for communion with the Divine. A sense of personal guilt had roused a sense of personal spiritual needs. By wild self-mortifications, and still wilder rites, men tried to wrestle their way into the presence of God, or to force Him to reveal Himself to them. In all this there was a good deal of imitation, both conscious and unconscious, of the fasts and mysteries of the Christians.

Under Septimius Severus persecution burst out again. The aggressiveness of Christians, especially as exhibited in such attacks as the 'Apologeticus' of Tertullian, may have provoked this; for Septimius was at first very friendly to the Church. In A.D. 202 a new edict was promulgated against them, and was put into force with great severity in Egypt and Africa. Clement left Alexandria, Origen's father was put to death, Perpetua and others suffered at Carthage. But this storm passed; and during the short reigns of Caracalla and Elagabalus the Church once more had comparative peace. Under Alexander Severus (222–235) it received even signs of favour. Both he and his mother Julia Mammæa were well disposed towards the Christians. Mammæa, while at Antioch, had conversations with Origen. But, although Severus is said to have wished to include Christ among Roman deities, he never caused Christianity to be made a *religio licita*. It was his confidential adviser Ulpian who in his 'De Officio Proconsulis' collected together the Imperial rescripts against the Christians, 'to teach,' as Lactantius says, 'how men ought to be punished who confess that they are worshippers of God.' But Alexander forbad prosecutions for high treason (*majestas*), and as Christians were often punished as *majestatis rei*, because they would not sacrifice to the Emperor, this was a great benefit to the Church.

The first barbarian Emperor expressed his detestation of his predecessor by reversing his policy, and he therefore renewed the persecutions. Maximin began by attacking the bishops, especially those to whom Alexander Severus had shown favour;

but afterwards earthquakes in Pontus and Cappadocia caused the popular fury to be directed against Christians in general. The persecutions, however, were local. It was possible to avoid them by moving into another district. Origen took refuge with Firmilian at Cæsarea in Cappadocia, and wrote his treatise 'On Martyrdom.' Pontianus, bishop of Rome, and Hippolytus were banished to Sardinia, where Pontianus died of ill-usage. But this trouble also passed away. Under the Gordians and Philip the Arabian the Christians were unmolested; and Philip is even said to have become a convert. Jerome says, *Primus omnium ex Romanis imperatoribus Christianus fuit*. But the story of his conversion is not probable. It may have grown out of his wishing, like Alexander Severus, to include Christ among recognised deities. Origen's silence respecting such an event as the conversion of the Emperor is almost conclusive; and this inference is confirmed by the fact that Philip did not legalise Christianity. Philip is another of the un-Roman Emperors of this period. These sovereigns live away from Rome and neglect Roman customs. Their religion is a foreign mixture and compromise—sometimes, as in the case of the sun-priest Elagabalus, nature-worship of the basest kind; sometimes, as with Alexander and Philip, a colourless Monotheism, in which all kinds of deities were recognised as partial expressions of the unseen universal power which pervades all things.

Just as the beneficent Alexander Severus was succeeded by the barbarous Maximin, so the not unfriendly Philip was followed by the unflinching Decius. With Decius begins the series of

<small>Crisis under Decius</small>

soldier Emperors, who commanded the armies rather than directed the government of the Empire, and who, being arbitrarily set up and violently cut down, seldom reigned for more than a few years at the utmost. In Decius we see a reaction, not merely from godless scepticism, but also against un-Roman religiousness and un-Roman profligacy. With him, as with M. Aurelius, the traditions of Rome were a dogma. He was an enthusiastic *laudator temporis acti*; and he failed, first, because his attempt came far too late, and secondly, because the troubled times were singularly unfavourable to it. His own private character was excellent. Wishing to be faithful to the high position thrust upon him, he selected Trajan as his model and assumed his name. To remedy the growing weakness of the Empire and the boundless corruption of morals, he determined to purify the Senate and make it once more efficient, to revive the ancient office of censor, under which luxury had been kept within bounds, and to restore the ancient religion, in the power of which Romans had controlled themselves and the world. The suppression of the Christians followed logically from this policy. No class of men had done more to bring about the general neglect of the ancestral gods; and, according to common report, no class of men were more flagrantly immoral. This matter had been trifled with too long, and decisive measures were imperative. The methods of Trajan and of M. Aurelius were no longer adequate. Rome had been growing weaker while this pestilent society increased and flourished. If Rome was to be restored to its old glory, Christianity must be exterminated.

Christianity, not the Christians. Decius was no Nero or Domitian wantonly delighting in cruelty and making an unpopular faith a means of obtaining victims. His policy was as conscientious as that of M. Aurelius, and far more thorough and consistent. He everywhere gave the Christians full opportunity to recant; and those who were willing to apostatise were not molested. Wherever the edict of A.D. 250 was published, an invitation to the Christians to sacrifice was the first step. Then followed threats, tortures, and either banishment with confiscation or imprisonment and death. At first death was seldom inflicted, excepting on bishops, against whom Decius was specially severe as ringleaders in mischief. Fabianus, bishop of Rome, was one of the first to suffer, and no successor was appointed for sixteen months. Cyprian ventures to assert that Decius would sooner have heard of a rival Emperor than of a new bishop of Rome. Alexander of Jerusalem and Babylas of Antioch both died in prison. But the cupidity of officials made them generally unwilling to kill their victims and thus destroy all chance of bribery. For certificates of having sacrificed were often bought by those who had not sacrificed, and many sent presents of money in the hope of buying off molestation. Nevertheless, the number of those who died after torture or under imprisonment was very great. Still greater was the number of those who either by open apostasy or unworthy evasions fell away from the faith. At first sight it appeared as if Decius would be successful. During the many intervals of peace the Gospel had received many nominal and

Christianity to be stamped out; if possib'e, without bloodshed

Wholesale apostasy

worthless adherents; and over these persecution gained an easy victory. People who had become Christians because Christianity was the fashion were not likely to suffer much for their creed when it ceased to be fashionable, or even safe. Dionysius of Alexandria thus describes what took place among his own flock: 'The decree arrived; in effect much like that foretold by the Lord, fraught with terror, such as, if it were possible, might cause even the elect to fall. But all were panic-stricken, and of those in high position many at once gave way, some of their own accord, some who held office induced by their employment, some dragged forward by their relations and friends. And as they were called by name they approached the impure and unholy sacrifices. Some were pale and trembling, as if they were about, not to sacrifice, but to be themselves sacrifices and victims to the idols, and they thus brought on themselves derision from the great crowd of bystanders, as it was quite plain that they were afraid of everything—afraid to die and afraid to sacrifice. Others with more readiness hurried to the altars and had the hardiness to maintain that not even in the past had they ever been Christians; concerning whom the declaration of the Lord is most true, that they shall scarcely be saved. Of the rest, some followed one of these two examples, some fled, and some were taken. Of these last, some held out as far as bonds and imprisonment; and some, after being shut up for several days, apostatised even before they came to the tribunal; while others, after having endured torture also for a while, in the end renounced Christ. But the firm and blessed pillars of the Lord, being made strong by Him, and receiving power and steadfastness in proportion to the mighty faith that was in them, became marvellous witnesses of his kingdom.' Cyprian writes of a similar state of things at Carthage and other large towns: ' They did not even wait to be arrested ere they went up; to be interrogated ere they denied. Before the battle many were conquered, and without ever meeting the enemy were cut down; and they did not even leave themselves this plea, that they appeared to sacrifice to idols unwillingly. Unasked they ran to the forum, of their own accord they hastened to death, as if all along they had been wishing for this, as if they were embracing an opportunity which they had always desired. How many had then to be put off by the magistrates because evening was coming on! How many even begged that their destruction might not be delayed! How can such an one plead violence as excusing his crime, when it was rather he himself who used violence to secure his ruin ? . . . And to many their own destruction was not enough. With mutual exhortations the people were urged on to utter ruin; death was pledged in turns in the deadly cup.'

Passages such as these seem to indicate that of those who did not save themselves by flight, a very large proportion—perhaps even the majority—fell away. There were many glorious martyrs and confessors; but those who either sacrificed or pretended that they had sacrificed were more numerous still. Yet it must not be assumed that flight was cowardice. It was obedience to Christ's command, and it involved great suffering. The fugitives lost all that they left behind, and had to endure grievous dangers and priva-

Flight and its consequences

tions in exile. Cyprian was among those who retired before the tempest; it was of the utmost importance to the Church of Carthage that he should continue to direct it in its difficulties. Dionysius of Alexandria and Cornelius of Rome did likewise. In Africa no bishops appear to have been executed; a few of them sacrificed, and the rest either escaped notice or fled. But both in sufferers and apostates the West was exceeded by the East.

The death of Decius caused a momentary pause, during which Cyprian held a Synod at Carthage. But Gallus soon renewed the persecutions by ordering special offerings to Apollo Salutaris for the withdrawal of a frightful pestilence. After his death there was again a cessation; for Valerian (253-260) was at first exceptionally kind to the Christians. In the Imperial household there was quite a congregation of them. When he was induced to change this policy he endeavoured to stamp out Christianity without bloodshed. He had been censor under Decius, and inherited the principles of his former master. He ordered that congregations should be deprived of their bishops and should be prevented from meeting. Public worship and prayers at the graves of the martyrs were forbidden. Under this edict Cyprian once more went into exile, and Xystus of Rome was put to death for visiting a cemetery. But its general effect was to turn banished bishops into missionaries, and this without depriving them of their influence over their flocks at home. Valerian then went much further. In 258 a second edict commanded that all bishops, presbyters, and deacons should be at once put to death; that all senators and

Valerian turns persecutor

magistrates should lose their property and rank, and then, if they refused to abjure Christ, should be put to death; that ladies were to lose their property and go into exile; and that members of the Imperial household who were *or had ever been* Christians were to be sent to work in chains on the Imperial estates. This edict, preserved for us by Cyprian in one of his last letters, is remarkable in three respects. (1) It is the first in which definite statutable punishments are assigned to the various classes of Christians. Hitherto the penalties had been at the discretion of the magistrates. (2) In this particular it formed a model for part of Diocletian's first edict. (3) It seems to pass over ordinary Christians of humble position. In the martyrdoms of this period we find the lower orders accompanying the martyrs with Christian sympathy and without fear or molestation; and we hear of very few *lapsi*. It was under this decree that the deacon Laurence of Rome, Cyprian, and several clergy of Carthage suffered.

Once more a persecutor was followed by a protector. Gallienus (260-268) was so favourable that he is commonly said to have made Christianity a *religio licita*. This has been disputed; but his action cannot mean much less. He ordered, says Eusebius, 'that the ministers of the word should perform their customary duties with freedom,' and that 'no one should molest them.' He also restored to the Christians the cemeteries, buildings, and lands which had been taken from them. He seems to have sent this order not only to Roman officials, but also to the chief officers of the Church—a fact which shows that bishops already had a recognised position in the world. And this time

<small>Formal to'eration under Gallienus</small>

of legally secured peace survived Gallienus. But in Aurelian (270–275), the successor nominated by Claudius Gothicus (268–270), we have an Emperor who, like Decius, interested himself in restoring reality to the worship of the national deities. This did not at first make him a persecutor; and we have seen him condescending to decide a Christian dispute, and deciding it in favour of the representatives of the Church (p. 33). But in 275 he determined on severe measures against these opponents of the gods of Rome, and had even signed an edict against them, when a conspiracy was formed against himself, and he was assassinated. Very few Christians suffered.

For forty-five years (from the capture of Valerian to Diocletian's persecution) the Christians had rest; and they needed it. The storm under Decius and Valerian had cleared the atmosphere; it had destroyed much that was rotten, and cleansed or washed away much that was impure and unwholesome. But it had also worked much destruction; and the Church had need of peace in which to repair the damage. Places of worship had to be rebuilt or refurnished. Interrupted discipline had to be restored. A gentle firmness was needed in dealing with those who had fallen in the persecutions, much tact and discretion in the treatment of those who had come out triumphant from them. The difficult combination of vigour with moderation was required all round. The world was still heathen, and must not be needlessly provoked. Persecution was still possible; and the lapsed, while condemned as grievous offenders, must not be driven to despair. Above all, Christians of all kinds needed to be taught that martyrdom is for the few, holiness for all; that suffering at the hands of the persecutor is not necessarily meritorious; and that in no case is death for Christianity a substitute for a Christian life. During these years of prosperity conversions were so frequent that large churches had to be erected in almost all the cities of the Empire.

The Imperial policy of Diocletian (A.D. 284-305) was to some extent a continuation of that of his predecessors; but in the main it was a new departure. Like them he aimed at a restoration of Roman greatness, a revival of the old Roman spirit that had conquered the world; but he aimed at it by different means. They had tried to bring back the past, and had hoped that by reviving the Senate and the censorship they could revive the moral forces which these institutions had at one time represented. Diocletian saw that worn-out and obsolete institutions, even if they could be restored to full vigour, were not adequate. What had suited Rome four or five centuries before was no standard for the Empire now. Galerius was more right than he himself knew, when he had proposed that it should be called not the Roman but the Dacian Empire. It was the army that ruled the Empire, and the army had ceased to be Roman; it was a motley host of Germans, Goths, Gauls, Africans, Greeks, and Persians. The Emperor of their choice was commonly not a Roman; and when he was elected he did not reign in Rome. Aurelian was an exception; but even he declined the old Roman palaces and lived in a villa of his own. Diocletian abandoned Rome altogether, and established a new capital in the East, with an Oriental court, marked by Oriental magnificence and ceremonial.

New departure under Diocletian

His scheme of government contained some grand ideas. There were to be two Emperors, of whom one was to be supreme, and two Cæsars who were to succeed the *Augusti* when either of them died or resigned; and the Emperors were not to reign for more than twenty years. This plan secured (1) division of the cares of government without division of the Empire; (2) a regular succession without the dangers of a dynasty; (3) an opening for ambitious and able men, who could become Cæsars without a revolution; (4) a safeguard against rebellion; for if one of the four was attacked the other three would protect him; (5) a safeguard against imbecile Emperors; for after twenty years each *Augustus* must resign. So long as the two Cæsars were content to remain subordinate to the two Emperors, and the second Emperor to the first, the scheme seemed to be not merely workable but strong. But the main feature of the whole remains behind. With statesmanlike sagacity Diocletian resolved that the scheme should have a religious basis. But what was to be the religion? While discarding the political forms of ancient Rome as obsolete, was he to wed his new constitution to the old religion which was equally obsolete? And here we are in doubt as to whether Diocletian believed that the Neo-Platonic heathenism which he adopted was a new form of religion adapted to his new constitution, or a bold restoration of the polytheism of ancient Rome. In any case he made the double mistake of supposing that, because religion may give life to the State, therefore the State can give life to religion, and of trying to compress into one reign a reformation which required centuries. And

His reconstruction of the Empire

THE PERSECUTIONS 185

it was Christianity which had the centuries. The religion which Diocletian preferred to it, to supply force and stability to his political system, was already a dead thing, galvanised into activity by the fanaticism of priests and philosophers, but having no hold on the hearts and consciences of the people. It remained for Constantine to remedy this fatal error by declaring for the one religion which could give strength and cohesion to the Empire.

Diocletian does not appear at first to have seen that his scheme led logically and necessarily to the suppression of Christianity. If the new constitution was to be based on the polytheism of ancient Rome, or upon the modern philosophic form of heathenism, how was it possible to maintain an attitude of toleration or neutrality towards a prevailing body of principles which was destructive of any such basis? Diocletian believed firmly in divination; and there is a story that he was at last induced to persecute by a priest who in his presence failed to obtain divination from the entrails of victims, and declared that the failure was due to the presence of impious · men, who, by means of the sign which the gods abhor, prevented the revelation from being made. The story may be literally true; but at any rate it represents the fact which confronted Diocletian—that paganism was becoming spellbound through the power of the Cross. No class of men felt this fact more keenly, or were more interested in bringing it home to the Emperor, than the pagan hierarchy. So long as persons in power believed in omens and divinations, sc long could those who interpreted such things have much

He is led on t_ perse- cute (1) by his own policy

(2) by the priests

influence. If Christianity succeeded in discrediting all pagan rites, all such influence was gone. The priests were supported by the Neo-Platonists, who contended that there was no reason why Christians should not coalesce with the popular religion. Let them worship the supreme God, but reverence the national deities as well. Originally there was no conflict between the gods and Christ, for Christ had never claimed to be God; that was a figment of the Apostles. Let the clergy be made to surrender this figment, and then Christian congregations would cease to reject the State religion. Hierocles, governor of Palmyra and afterwards Vicarius of Bithynia, was an exponent of such views. He wrote a treatise called 'The Lover of Truth,' which, although in form an attempt to reason with the Christians, was in reality a bitter attack on them on the lines of Celsus. It is lost, but we have the reply of Eusebius to it. Hierocles is said to have done much towards bringing about the persecution, and to have been specially brutal in putting the edicts into execution in Bithynia.

(3) by the philosophers

It was in the Cæsar Galerius that the persecuting party found an agent ready to work their will. He had risen from a herdsman to be a general and then a prince; but beyond his military ability he had no gifts, either moral or intellectual. In spite of his marriage with Valeria, the almost Christian daughter of Diocletian, he remained an implacable and fanatical pagan. Under the influence of his mother, a devotee of Phrygian orgies, and Theotecnus, a Neo-Platonic theosophist, he espoused the policy of persecution, and urged Diocletian to make a strenuous effort to

(4) by Galerius and his mother

stamp out Christianity. For various reasons the Emperor was most unwilling to acquiesce. He was averse to cruelty and to a reversal of the policy of the last forty years—a policy which he had himself supported for nearly twenty years. He had numerous Christians about his person in the palace at Nicomedia, and was well served by them. All previous attempts to crush the Christians had failed, and they were stronger than ever now. To persecute them would cause disturbance throughout the whole Empire, and after much bloodshed nothing would be effected. All experience showed that Christians were not afraid to die. But he gave his consent to a military order that all soldiers should attend the sacrifices; an order which caused many persons, both officers and privates, to leave the army. This would be specially exasperating to Galerius, who was an ardent soldier. How was the service to be carried on if such desertions were allowed? He urged Diocletian to consult a few leading men, among them Hierocles, the author of the 'truth-loving' attack on Christianity. This council recommended persecution. Diocletian, still unconvinced and uneasy, finally consulted the oracle of Apollo at Miletus. Its reply reminds us of the Cretan who said that the Cretans are always liars. The god declared that he could not speak the truth because of the Christians. This was of course understood to mean that the Christians must be suppressed, and Diocletian could hold out no longer. There was probably nothing that he believed in more firmly than in soothsaying and oracles; and, even if he doubted the truth of the response, to have acted on the doubt would have been a public disavowal of the State religion. Over-talked, and perhaps half convinced, he gave an unwilling consent to the policy of 'the Evil Beast' and his mother; but declared that he would have no bloodshed. An argument that may, perhaps, have weighed strongly with Diocletian, was the fact that in two years' time he would cease to be Augustus, and Galerius would take his place. Better allow the persecution to take place while he could keep it within bounds, than leave it for Galerius to carry it out without check. Years afterwards the retired Emperor explained to the father of the historian Vopiscus how sovereigns were hoodwinked and made the tools of their ministers. 'Good and cautious as he may be, the best of emperors is sold.'

The Feast of the *Terminalia*, February 23, 303, was chosen as the day for placing a terminus to the Christian religion. It proved the terminus of Imperial paganism. At 'the Destruction of the Churches,' the heathen establishment was buried in the ruins. At dawn the prefect went to the great Church of Nicomedia, one of the ornaments of the city, and broke open the doors. His party were surprised at finding no image of God in it. They set fire to the service-books and fittings, and levelled the building to the ground. The Christians had twenty-four hours to consider this hint of what was coming, and then the Imperial edict which revoked the order of Gallienus was posted. All churches were to be razed to the ground. All sacred books of the Christians were to be destroyed. All officials who were Christians were to be degraded and deprived of civil rights; and all other free Christians were to be reduced to the condition of

First edict of Diocletian

slaves. This meant that all were outlaws, and were liable to torture. Those who were slaves already were to lose all hope of being set free. The religious gatherings of Christians had been illegal from the time of Trajan to that of Gallienus, but it was a new thing to proscribe their buildings. It was also quite a new thing to proscribe their sacred writings. The remainder of the edict was on the lines of that of Valerian. It fixed definite penalties; and, severe as these were, they were a protection against the cruelty and caprice of magistrates. It omits three provisions of Valerian's edict. There is no special penalty for clergy, or for ladies, or for members of the Imperial household. On the other hand, it covers ordinary Christians of no rank or position. It shows consummate ability. The intention was to reduce Christianity at once to insignificance by destroying the public evidences of its existence and influence; to render it in time impossible by cutting off its life-springs; and meanwhile to frighten existing Christians into submission by threats and penalties. Without its mysteries and Scriptures Christianity must starve; and severity to its adherents would hasten its dissolution. In all this we trace the skill of the statesman and the moderation of one who desires to carry out a severe measure in the quickest and most merciful way. The edict was at once torn down by a Christian, who was forthwith arrested and roasted to death for this audacious act of high treason.

We shall probably never know the truth about the two fires in the palace at Nicomedia. One or both may have been accidental; and years afterwards Constantine, who was there, said that the

Two fires at Nicomedia

first was caused by lightning. One or both may have been contrived by Galerius to throw suspicion upon the Christians. One or both may really have been the work of fanatical Christians. Perhaps the first was an accident, and then Galerius, finding it useful as a charge against the Christians, contrived a second in order to augment the feeling against them. Anyhow, he absented himself from the investigation. Although it was the depth of winter, he set off for his Danubian provinces, declaring that *he* was not going to stay in Nicomedia to be burned alive by the Christians. After the first fire the household slaves, whether Christians or not, were tortured; after the second the heathen seem to have been passed over. In the second case Diocletian began with his own wife, Prisca, and her daughter Valeria, the wife of Galerius, who were preparing for baptism. To confirm their innocence of the supposed Christian plot, they consented to offer sacrifice.

While the edict was being promulgated throughout the Empire, civil disturbances broke out at Antioch and in Melitene. It was supposed that exasperated Christians were concerned in them, and that a general rising might be impending. A serious internal trouble of this kind would be a signal to the enemies of the Empire to attack it. Diocletian determined on decisive measures. The first edict, unlike Valerian's, had taken no special notice of the clergy. In a general rising they would, of course, be the leaders; and in any case, to get them out of the way would hasten the dissolution of Christianity. Diocletian put forth a second edict, that all the clergy, of

Second edict

whatever rank, were to be at once imprisoned. Forthwith there was no room in the prisons for criminals. Every cell was crowded with clerics, including readers and exorcists, who were to be kept as hostages for the good behaviour of the congregations. Valerian had tried banishing the bishops; and that had turned them into missionaries, while it left them free to govern their dioceses by letter. He had then tried putting them to death; and that had kindled enthusiasm without going even near to exterminating them. Diocletian's policy of turning them into hostages was much more statesmanlike; and it was a policy which could be revoked whenever it ceased to be advantageous. Dead clergy could neither be restored nor deprived of their influence as martyrs. Owing to the unequal means of communication between different parts of the Empire, it sometimes happened that the second edict arrived almost, if not quite, as soon as the first. In some cases friendly hands delayed the publication: and the two were carried into effect with very different degrees of rigour in different parts of the Empire. As already stated, Constantius in Gaul did little more than order the destruction of a few churches; and, speaking generally, the persecution in the *West* lasted for barely two years. But Maximian in Italy and Africa, and Galerius in the East, made the most of their opportunities of inflicting suffering. Maximian delighted in cruelty, and Galerius had a fanatical hatred of Christians. The accounts of the tortures inflicted in their dominions are appalling.

Diocletian had declared that he would have no bloodshed, and neither edict imposed the penalty of death on any class of Christians. But the first edict gave ample opportunity to the persecutor who was disposed to be bloodthirsty. It made no provision for the treatment of those Christians who refused to deliver up the sacred books. Consequently it was possible to proceed to any extremities against such persons, as sorcerers who possessed books of magic, or as rebels who set Imperial orders at defiance. Once more we have to lament the effects of a long interval of prosperity. Some at once abjured Christianity; others, to save themselves from molestation, surrendered the Scriptures to destruction. Persons who compromised themselves in this way were known as *traditores*, and they ranked as a new class of unfaithful Christians along with the *lapsi*, who had sacrificed, and the *libellatici*, who had bought certificates of having done so. Others, again, when asked to give up the Scriptures, gave up other books, which were accepted as the Scriptures. Roman officials were sometimes quite willing to be deceived in this way. 'We must have some books to burn; give us copies that you don't want.' It became a question whether Christians who had practised this *ruse* were to be classed as *traditores* or not. And among those who would condescend to nothing of the kind, the motives which induced them to withstand, and even needlessly to provoke, the persecutors, were often sadly mixed or altogether faulty. Some who were in hopeless troubles chose this as an honourable way of getting free from the burden of life. Others hoped by a voluntary sacrifice of life to atone for a career of wickedness. Even among those who did not court persecution there was often an arrogant tone

[margin note: Working of the two edicts]

of defiance, an offensive abuse of the presiding magistrate, and a confident assertion of their powers of endurance more in harmony with the spirit of a Red Indian savage than with that of a Christian martyr. Of the effects of locking up the clergy we have little information. No doubt many escaped imprisonment and administered the sacraments in secret. But the horrors that took place under these and subsequent edicts were such that to this day the Coptic Churches date from the accession of Diocletian (A.D. 284) as 'the Era of the Martyrs.' And one effect of the first edict has been permanent. The wholesale destruction of the copies of the Scriptures caused the extinction of many ancient and independent texts. When the storm passed, copies were made rapidly from surviving MSS. The result was that a composite text emanating from Constantinople got possession of the field, and became the dominant form in which the Greek Testament was known to Christians. This composite text is the basis of the corrupt *Textus Receptus*, and is in the main the text used by our translators in the Authorised Version of 1611.

But the horrors of 'the Era of the Martyrs' were not yet at an end. In December 303 Diocletian celebrated his *Vicennalia* to commemorate the twentieth anniversary of his accession. The usual edict for the release of prisoners was published with a note stating that this included the Christian clergy, *provided that they would sacrifice*; if they refused, *they might be subjected to any kind of torture*. An ingenious writer, who contends that 'there was nothing in the first edict to constitute a persecution,' informs us that

Third edict

this third edict ' was intended as a special act of mercy to the Christian Church.' It is a strange way of defending Diocletian to maintain that he could pull down the Churches, burn the Bibles and Prayer-books, and reduce the congregations to slavery, without knowing that he was persecuting; and that he could believe that he was being specially merciful in giving imprisoned clergy the alternative of apostasy or torture. The result was again distressing. A few months of imprisonment—doubtless accompanied by many sufferings—had demoralised the majority of the clergy. Eusebius tells us that, although very many stood firm, yet 'thousands,' either before or after torture, sacrificed. At Antioch only one man remained in prison, and he was tortured till he died. Almost immediately after publishing the third edict Diocletian was struck by a kind of paralysis, and it is doubtful whether he had any share in the fourth edict which was put out in his name in 304, just a year before he abdicated.

The question is not a very important one; but we have our choice of four hypotheses. (1) Diocletian was in a state of temporary imbecility, and Maximian ventured to put out this tremendous edict without even consulting him. (2) With his mind somewhat unhinged he sanctioned the edict. (3) He had become so exasperated by the trouble caused by the Christians that he now persecuted with a will. (4) The extraordinary success of the third edict induced him to believe that with an increase of severity Christianity might very soon be exterminated. The purport of the edict was this—that in every town every person without exception should be required to offer sacrifice and

Fourth edict

also pour libations to the idols; and that those who refused should be put to death and their property be confiscated. Along with this came the infamous rescript against virginity, which rendered it possible to send maidens who refused to apostatise to be outraged in the public brothels; and from the evidence of Eusebius, Chrysostom, and Ambrose, as well as from the Acts of various martyrs, it is clear that this diabolical order was frequently put in force. Just as the persecuting edicts often kindled a new enthusiasm for Christianity, so did this kindle an increased enthusiasm for celibacy. But here also evil was mingled with the good. The enthusiasm too often became fanatical; and such extravagant value was placed upon mere external purity that some women defeated the rescript by suicide, and found plenty of Christians to applaud this grievous mistake.

Galerius kept Diocletian to the terms of the constitution, and both he and Maximian abdicated, May 1, 305. This left Galerius and Constantius Emperors; and the new Cæsars were Severus and Maximin Daza. When Constantius died a year later at York, Severus became Augustus, while Constantine, to the disgust of Galerius, became the new Cæsar. October 28, 306, Maxentius was elected Emperor by the troops and people of Rome, and he recalled his father Maximian to power. Severus opposed him and was killed. But the father and son could not agree. Maximian, like Galerius and Maximin, was for persecution; Maxentius was for popularity. 'At the beginning of his reign,' says Eusebius, 'Maxentius feigned our faith *to please and flatter the people*; and he ordered his

[margin: Abdication of Diocletian]

servants to leave off the persecution against the Christians, putting on a form of godliness.' The son proved the stronger, and Maximian had to leave Rome; but the dispute shows us how far we are now from the time when the masses clamoured for outrages on the Christians. Maximian fortified himself by an alliance with Constantine, to whom he offered the title of Augustus. This violation of the constitution of Diocletian was in 308 ratified by Galerius, who had himself been guilty of a worse violation in making Licinius Emperor of the West, although he had never been Cæsar. Maximin also was made Augustus. So the Empire had now six Emperors: Galerius, Maxentius, Maximian, Licinius, Constantine, and Maximin. In order to cover his own usurpation Maximian wished Diocletian to resume the purple; and Galerius also wished to have the support of Diocletian's great name. 'I wish,' was the famous reply, ' that you could see the kitchen-garden laid out by my own hands at Salona; you would, I am sure, admit that what you propose ought never to be risked.' Planting cabbages was more satisfactory work than trying to root out Christianity.

It was probably in 308 that the edict against the Manicheans was issued at Alexandria, March 31, by Maximin and Galerius. But the year and other details are open to discussion. It agreed with the first edict against the Christians in fixing definite penalties, and in ordering the writings of the sect to be burned; but the penalties in this case included death to the leaders and promoters. At the same time instructions seem to have been given that the penalty of death was to be sparingly employed in

Fifth edict

the case of Christians. But this relaxation was of short duration. Maximin, supported probably by Galerius, issued the fifth edict against the Church, ordering the restoration of all idols in public places; the participation of all persons in sacrifices and libations, care being taken that every one *tasted* the offerings; and the sprinkling of all articles sold in the markets and of all persons entering the public baths with sacrificial liquids. Eusebius tells us that the heathen themselves condemned this malicious edict in no measured terms. But there were plenty of officials ready to carry out these directions, and martyrdoms of the most hideous kinds continued to be frequent. It was in Maximin's dominions that between A.D. 308 and 311 hundreds of Christians were *as a special mercy* merely deprived of the right eye and lamed in the left leg, instead of being tortured to death.

In February 310 Maximian tried to assassinate Constantine. He was caught, thanks to his daughter Fausta, whom he had induced Constantine to marry, and was hanged. Next spring Galerius, attacked by a loathsome disorder, issued his edict of toleration, one of the most extraordinary documents that ever was penned. It reviles the Christians as obstinate dissenters, who have deserted the ancient faith and have been punished that they might return to it. Salutary punishment having in many cases failed to convert them, prompt indulgence shall now be shown. Christianity may once more be practised *provided they do nothing to break the discipline.* In return for this it will be their duty to pray for the good health of the Emperor and the Empire. Thus it insults the character and

Galerius's edict of toleration

intelligence of the Christians by calling them apostates and asking them to believe that the persecutions have been prompted by benevolence; and it then bargains with them for their prayers by promising them toleration. And the promised toleration is qualified by a clause which can be used at any moment to retract it. Moreover, there is a studied ambiguity about the alleged apostasy of the Christians; it may mean desertion either of the old polytheism or of pure Apostolic tradition. The edict was posted April 30, 311, at Nicomedia. In less than a month Galerius died. But the decree had the support of Constantine and Licinius, and produced much improvement in the condition of the Christians. Licinius cared nothing about Christianity or its adherents, but he hated the philosophers who had preached persecution. Constantine's name was prefixed to the edict, probably without his consent. Had he been consulted, a more generous measure would have been the result. Maximin's name was not added. Either he refused his consent, or Galerius did not venture to ask it. But even Maximin sent instructions to the officials under him that they need not continue the persecution; Christians going to public worship were not to be molested. Many of the magistrates, sick of the bloody work, went beyond these instructions. From prisons, mines, and various hiding-places, multitudes of Christians, many of them still marked with wounds and scars, flocked back, singing hymns of praise, to enjoy the privileges of a common worship. Even the heathen in some cases expressed their sympathy.

Their rejoicing was gall and wormwood to Maximin and the philosophers. An anti-Christian agitation was once more got up. Addresses, probably at Maximin's own instigation, were composed at Antioch and elsewhere, praying him to grant 'local option' to the cities, empowering the majority to expel the Christians, who were a public nuisance, from among them. Theotecnus, Curator of Antioch, who seems to have been an apostate, took the lead in this agitation. It included another attempt to revive paganism on lines borrowed from the Church. A pagan hierarchy was organised, with defined districts like dioceses and parishes. Parodies of baptism and the Eucharist were instituted, sham miracles were worked, and sham oracles uttered. Daily services were provided; and those who neglected the public worship were liable to severe penalties. It was the nearest approach to a pagan Church that had yet been made. And it was accompanied by a new literary attack on Christianity. The old calumnies were furbished up again. Prostitutes were suborned to bring charges of abominable practices among Christians. Their lying 'revelations' were taken down, and Maximin forthwith gave orders that these should be placarded in every city in the Empire. But the most cunning device of all was the forgery of the 'Acts of Pilate.' This again was a plagiarism from the Christians. For a hundred and fifty years Christians had appealed to the evidence of documents which bore the name of Pilate. Theotecnus had probably seen some of these, and had seen that such things could be invented just as easily to discredit Christianity as to support it. He made one clumsy mistake, which Eusebius pointed out. He placed the Crucifixion five years before Pilate became Procurator of Judæa. But this passed unnoticed by the multitude. The work has perished, but it was 'full of every kind of blasphemy against Christ,' and probably turned the whole history of the Passion into ridicule. This was not only posted up in the cities, but copies of it were sent to all the schools in the East and in Egypt, and the masters were ordered to see that the boys learned it by heart. Those who know how garbage of this kind is devoured and remembered by the children of East London at the present day will be able to judge of the results of this diabolical stratagem. Not only were Christian ears everywhere tortured by the mocking recitations of these youthful blasphemers, but in the rising generation the feelings of reverence and awe were poisoned at their very source. Amid such influences it was only natural that Christians should again have to suffer a great deal of molestation, and in some cases even death.

But the end was at hand. October 28, 312, the anniversary of his accession, Maxentius was defeated by Constantine at the Milvian Bridge, and in his flight was drowned in the Tiber. Soon after the victory Constantine and Licinius put forth the edict of toleration which proclaimed religious liberty throughout the Empire. It is not a matter of much moment how this was done. The common view is that one edict was published in 312, and a second—the famous Edict of Milan, referring to the former one—in 313. But it is quite possible that the Edict of Milan was published in 312, and that the previous edict to which it refers is not the supposed earlier edict of Constantine and Licinius, but that of Galerius, Constantine, and Licinius in 311. It is of more importance to notice the character of this

Edict of Milan

final Toleration Act. The Edict of Milan forms an epoch in the history of religion. It is the Great Charter of liberty of conscience. Its principles have often been violated and often reaffirmed, but they have never been surpassed. Gallienus had practically made Christianity a *religio licita*; it was one of the numerous forms of worship allowed by the State. Diocletian had unwillingly withdrawn this privilege. Galerius had, equally unwillingly, and in ambiguous terms, restored it. The Edict of Milan did a great deal more than restore Christianity to its full privileges as a *religio licita*; it promoted *all* religions to the same rank. To be a *religio licita* ceased to be a privilege; it was a right allowed to all. It was laid down as a principle that the State 'has no business to refuse freedom of religion; and that to the judgment and desire of each individual must be left the power of seeing to matters of belief according to the man's own free will.' Polytheism of every kind, Manicheism, Judaism, Gnosticism, Montanism, and Catholicism, were all made equal in the eyes of the law. The conscience of the individual was henceforth to be the sole arbiter in such matters. Thus ten years of bitter persecution had ended in the victory, not merely of the persecuted Christian faith, but of the outraged human conscience.

It is impossible to form any trustworthy estimate of the number of the martyrs. The arguments which have been used to prove that the total amount was something quite inconsiderable do not carry conviction. The probabilities are decidedly the other way. No doubt the Christian accounts which have come down to us contain many exaggerations as

Number of martyrs

regards both numbers and details. On the other hand, numerous authentic accounts have perished; and in very many instances no record was ever made. It would be quite unreasonable to suppose that the evidence which has come down to us covers anything like the whole area. There is no improbability in supposing that 'the half was not told.' Even in the case of large towns we are often in ignorance respecting the working of the edicts; and what may have taken place in obscure districts is a matter of pure conjecture. Clement of Alexandria speaks of 'copious streams of martyrs' blood shed daily,' at a time when under Commodus there was no special edict out against the Christians, but only the edict of Trajan, which the fanaticism of a magistrate or of the mob could at any moment put in action. The burden of proof rests with those who maintain that, whereas we have contemporary evidence respecting numerous martyrdoms in certain places, few or no martyrdoms took place in those parts respecting which no such evidence exists. Justin Martyr is only one of many who were led to the conviction that Christianity was true by seeing the constancy with which Christians suffered for their belief. The rapid progress of the Gospel between A.D. 260 and 303, and the rapid conversion of the Empire under Constantine, are more intelligible if we suppose that numerous martyrdoms under Decius and Valerian in the one case, and under Diocletian in the other, were among the causes of it. 'The seed of blood was scattered: there arose the harvest of the Church.'

But it would be a grave error to suppose that accurate statistics would give us the full measure of the suffering inflicted. The miseries of those awful times are not to be reckoned by any tabulated account of burnings, crucifixions, hangings, decapitations, crushings, scourgings, mutilations, rackings, scrapings, brandings, degradations, imprisonments, banishments, and confiscations. Frightful as such tables would be, they would leave undescribed and indescribable the exquisite agony of living for years in hourly apprehension, for oneself and all dearest to one, of things far worse than death. And the torture of this ceaseless anxiety was not alone. Along with it came the miserable feeling of suspicion towards those among whom one lived. Every one was a possible spy or traitor. Masters and slaves, brothers and sisters, parents and children, husbands and wives, informed against one another with sickening frequency. A man's foes were those of his own household. Whether we count the actual deaths, or the physical tortures, or the constant dread of betrayal and arrest, a time of persecution is indeed a 'Reign of Terror.'

The Reign of Terror

But the terrors of three centuries won a triumph for all time. Of both persecuted and persecutors the saying proved true: παθήματα μαθήματα. To the Christians these sufferings were discipline; to the heathen they were instruction. Purified by these fires, the Christians purified the world, and, like their Master, conquered by dying. 'And this is the victory that overcometh the world, even our faith.'

The victory

INDEX.

ABERCIUS

ABERCIUS and his epitaph, 47
Accusations against Christians, 144
Acts of Martyrs, 195
— — Pilate, 199
Adaptability of Christianity, 19
Ælia or Jerusalem, 24
Africa, Churches in, 108
Africanus, Julius, 78, 81
Alexander, conquests of, 14
— of Jerusalem, 22, 67
— Severus, 174, 175
Alexandria, characteristics of, 61
Alexandrian Schools, 62
Allegorising interpretation, 71, 77, 83
Ambrose, friend of Origen, 78, 81
Anicetus and Polycarp, 40, 92
Antioch, Church of, 27
— Councils at, 33
— School of, 34
Antipopes, 98
Antoninus Pius, 168
Apollinaris, Claudius, 49
Apollonius and Montanism, 37
— of Tyana, 173
— the Martyr, 171
Apologies, 55, 145
— effect of the, 158
— typical, 159

BEDE

Apologists, Greek, 147, 154
— Latin, 155
Apostasy frequent, 101, 106, 122, 124, 137, 177, 192
Apostles, work of, 8
Appeal to Aurelian, 33, 182
— — tradition, 58, 66, 91, 94, 95
Aristides, 55, 149
Arles, Council at, 104, 141, 143
Arnobius, 129, 155
Artemon, 52
Asia Minor, Churches in, 35
— — and Gaul, 131
Athanasius, 84. 89
Athenagoras, 55
Athens, Church of, 54
Augustine on persecutions, 160
— — Tertullianists, 116
Aurelian decides a Christian dispute, 33, 182
Aurelius, Marcus, 169, 171
Authorities for this period, vii

BABYLAS, 30, 177
Bacchylus of Corinth, 60
Baptism of heretics, 104, 125
Barcochba, revolt of, 23, 147, 165
Bede's story of Lucius, 139

BITHYNIA

Bithynia, 4, 53, 165
Britain, Christianity in, 138
British Church insignificant, 142
—— distinct from the English, 143
Buddhism and Christianity, 19

CÆCILIAN of Carthage, 128
Cæsarea in Palestine, 24
—— Cappadocia, 26, 32
Caius, 97
Callistus and Hippolytus, 100
Canon of Scripture, 52
Caracalla, 78
Carthage, characteristics of, 109
— Councils of, 119, 124, 125
Catechetical School, 64
Causes of the triumph of Christianity, 14, 17
Celsus and Origen, 13, 159
Cemeteries, 180
Charges against Christians, 144, 150
Christianity aggressive, 152, 161, 174
— Divine, 20
Christians, name of, 27
Church Universal, 1, 19
Churches, autonomy of ancient, 88
Classical literature, 145
Claudius Apollinaris, 49
— Gothicus, 182
Clement of Alexandria, 30, 56, 66
—— Rome, 56, 89
Commentaries, 51, 65, 78
Commodus and the Church, 96, 171
Constantine, 195, 198, 200
— in Gaul, 137
Constantius, 136, 195
— moderation of, 137
Corinth, Church of, 56, 89
Council at Antioch, 32
—— Arles, 104, 141, 143
—— Carthage, 119, 124, 125

EDICT

Council at Iconium, 104
—— Rimini, 142
—— Rome, 107
Cyprian, 119, 180, 181
— rebukes Stephen, 103, 136
— flight of, 121
— greatness of, 127
— martyrdom of, 126

DECIUS, character of, 176
— persecution under, 121, 177
Demetrius of Alexandria, 75, 79
Diffusion of Christianity, 3, 8, 13, 202
Diocletian, aims of, 183
— constitution of, 184
— driven to persecute, 185, 188
— edicts of, 188, 190
— resignation of, 195
Diognetus, Epistle to, 6, 156
Dionysius the Areopagite, 54
— of Alexandria, 81, 84, 178
—— Corinth, 59
—— Rome, 84, 105
Disputes about Easter, 36, 40, 92, 96
—— *Lapsi*, 102, 124
—— rebaptism, 104, 125
Divine origin of Christianity, 20
Döllinger, 98, 100, 106
Domitian, persecution under, 165
Donatists, 104, 106, 107, 128
Dorotheus, 33, 34

EASTER controversies, 36, 60, 92, 96
Ebionites, 24, 45
Ecclesiastical Latin, 114
Edict of Aurelius, 169
—— Decius, 177
—— Galerius, 197
—— Gallienus, 165, 181
—— Maximin Daza, 197

EDICT

Edict of Milan, 200
— — Trajan, 166
— — Valerian, 180
Edicts of Constantine, 198, 200
— — Diocletian, 188, 190, 193
Edict against Manicheism, 196
Egypt, antiquity of, 62
— conversion of, 87
Emperor, worship of, 15, 24, 151, 174
Encroachments of Rome, 36, 96, 103
English Church distinct from the British, 143
Ephesus, Church of, 35, 36
Episcopacy, 92
' Era of Martyrs,' 193
Evidences of Christianity, 159
Eusebius of Cæsarea, 26

FANATICISM, Christian, 42, 122, 128
Fires at Nicomedia, 189
Firmilian of Cæsarea, 32, 81, 125, 175
— condemns Stephen, 104
Flight from persecution, 67, 75, 121, 179
Florinus, Epistle to, 40, 132
Forged writings, 156, 199
Fourth Gospel, Asiatic evidence for, 53, 132, 133

GALERIUS, 186, 190, 197
Gallican Church Asiatic, 131
Gallienus, 25, 165
Gaul, persecutions in, 136, 171
Gibbon's five causes, 9
— unfairness, 11, 127
Gnosticism, 36, 46, 58
Greek Christianity, 88
— Bishops of Rome. 89
— language, 15
Gregory Thaumaturgus, 60
— of Tours, 54, 135

LAPSI

HADRIAN and Alexandria, 62
— — the Jews, 23
— — the Christians, 149, 158, 168
Heathen morals, 17, 172
— philosophy, 16, 173
— polemics, 144, 199
Heathenism, revival of, 172, 199
Hegesippus, 59, 91
Heresy, 58, 91
Heretics, baptism of, 104, 125
Hermias, 150, 154
Hierapolis, Church of, 44
Hierocles, 186, 187
Hierópolis, 47
Hippolytus, 97, 172, 175
— an Antipope, 98
— and Origen, 77, 99

IDEALS of the Church, v
Idolatry, 153
Ignatius of Antioch, 27
— his Epistle to Rome, 90
Interpretation of Scripture, 34, 71, 77, 73
Irenæus, 4, 94, 154
— and Polycarp, 40, 132
— condemns Florinus, 40, 132
— — Victor, 37, 96

JEROME on ecclesiastical writers, viii
— — Origen, 73
— — Tertullian, 112
Jerusalem, Church of, 21
— destruction of, 14
Jews, bitterness of, 23, 41
— controversy with, 147
Justin Martyr, 4, 53, 70, 92, 150, 158, 169

LACTANTIUS, 155, 160, 174
Lapsi, 102, 107, 124, 181, 182, 192

LATIN

Latin apologists, 155
— Christianity, 89
— ecclesiastical, 114
Lay preaching, 78
Leonides, 73, 74
Libellatici, 122, 124
Libelli pacis, 123
Libraries, 22, 26, 61
Licinius, 196, 200
Literary activity in the second century, 49, 51
Literature, classical, 145
Lucian of Antioch, 34
— the satirist, 31, 172
Lucius, Bede's story of, 139
Lyons, Church of, 131

MACEDONIAN conquests, 14
Mahometanism, 19
Mammæa, 173, 174
Manicheism, Edict against, 196
Marcellinus, apostasy of, 106
Marcia and the Christians, 96, 171
Marcion, 40, 92
M. Aurelius, character of, 169
—— persecution under, 131, 171
Marinus, martyrdom of, 25
Martyrs, extravagances of, 122
— honours paid to, 123, 128
— numbers of, 127, 201
Maxentius, 195, 200
Maximian, 136, 191, 195, 197
Maximin the Thracian, 174
Maximin Daza, 195, 196
Melchiades, 106
Melito of Sardis, 50, 171
Mensurius of Carthage, 128
Milman on Gibbon, 9
Minucius Felix, 4, 89
Miracles, 156
Missions seldom mentioned, 66
Montanism, 49, 96, 97, 212
Morality of Christians, 12, 152, 156
—— heathen, 16, 146
—— the Gospel, 20

PHILIP

Mysteries, heathen, 16, 153, 172, 173, 199

NAME of Christian, 27
Neoplatonism, 173
Nero, persecution under, 165, 177
Newman on Gibbon, 11
—— Origen, 83
Nicæa, Council of, 24, 79, 126
Nicomedia, 183, 189
Noëtus, 100
Novatian, 101
Novatus, 102
Number of martyrs, 127, 201

ORDINATION by presbyters, 87
Origen at Alexandria, 75, 78
—— Cæsarea, 26, 80
—— Rome, 77
—— Tyre, 81
— characteristics of, 81
— errors of, 83
— greatness of, 72, 82
— and Hippolytus, 77, 99
—— Tertullian, 100
Original sources, vii

PAGAN objections, 150, 164
— society, 15, 156
Paganism, revival of, 172, 199
— strength of, 162
Pamphilus, 25, 26
Pantænus, 64
Papias, 43
— and St. Paul, 45
Paschal controversies, 36, 40, 60, 92
Paul of Samosata, 30
Persecutions, causes of, 161
— fallacies about, 164
— nature of, 171, 177, 191
— number of, 160
Petrine claims, 33, 57, 89, 91, 93, 94, 97, 105
Philip the Arabian, 81, 175

PHILOSOPHY

Philosophy and Christianity, 63, 70, 76, 80, 154
Pilate, Acts of, 199
Pionius, 38
Pliny the Younger, 4, 6, 165
Polycarp, 38
— and Anicetus, 40, 92
— — Ignatius, 39
— — Irenæus, 40
Polycrates and Victor, 36, 96
Pontius's Life of Cyprian, 126
Pontus, 4
Pope, title of, 63, 101, 121
Pothinus of Lyons, 132
Presbyterian ordination, 87
Prophecy, argument from, 155

QUADRATUS, 55, 149
Quartadecimans, 36, 40, 92, 96
Quintus the Apostate, 42

REBAPTISM, 104, 125
Revival of paganism, 172, 199
Roman encroachments, 36, 96
— Law a *pædagogus*, 15
— organisation, 14
— religion, 15
Rome, Bishops of, 33, 57, 85, 89, 91, 93
— Church of, 88, 94, 96, 105
— clergy of, 102

SACRIFICATI, 122, 124
Schism of Hippolytus, 98
— — Montanus, 49
— — Novatian, 101
— — Tertullian, 112
School of Alexandria, 62
— — Antioch, 34
Severus, Alexander, 174, 175
— Septimius, 158, 174
— Sulpicius, 131
C. H.

VALERIA

Smyrna, Church of, 38
Socrates on Origen, 84
Soul, theories about the, 112
Sources, historical, vii
Spread of Christianity, 3, 8, 13, 162, 202
Stephen and Cyprian, 103, 125
Syria, Churches in, 21, 35
Syrian text, 34

TATIAN, 92, 154
Terror, Reign of, 202
Tertullian, 5, 6, 95, 99, 111, 155, 160
— language of, 114
— schism of, 112
— and Cyprian, 119
— — Origen, 99
— — Rome, 100
Text of Scripture, 34, 193
Theoctistus of Cæsarea, 25, 78
Theophilus of Antioch, 29
Theotecnus of Cæsarea, 25
— — Antioch, 199
Thurificati, 122
Toleration, Edicts of, 165, 181, 197, 200
— Roman, 163
— universal, 201
Torture, 164, 189, 191, 193
Tradition, 58, 66, 91, 94, 95
Traditores, 192
Trajan, Edict of, 166, 167, 169, 202

ULPIAN, 174
Universal religion, 2, 19, 53
— toleration, 201
Un-Roman Emperors, 174

VACANCIES at Rome, 101, 106
Valeria, 186, 190

P

VALERIAN

Valerian, persecution under, 105, 126, 180
Victor and Polycrates, 36, 96
Vienne, persecution at, 131, 171
Virginity, Rescript against, 195

WORSHIP of the Emperor, 15, 24, 151, 174

ZEAL

Writers, ancient, vii
— Modern, viii

XYSTUS, 105, 126, 180

ZEAL of converts, 11, 12
— — martyrs, 122

www.ingramcontent.com/pod-product-compliance
Lightning Source LLC
Chambersburg PA
CBHW021829230426
43669CB00008B/918